Christopher Fremantle

December 17, 1906–December 19, 1978

Christopher Fremantle

ON ATTENTION

talks, essays and letters
based on the ideas of
G.I. GURDJIEFF

Edited by
LILLIAN FIRESTONE BOAL

First Edition
second printing

Copyright © 1993 by Indications Press

Printed in the United States of America

Published by, and available from, Indications Press, 45 Thurmont Road, Denville, NJ 07834

All rights reserved under International and Pan American Copyright Conventions. No part of this publication may be reproduced in any form or by any means, electronic or mechanical, including photocopy, recording, or any information storage and retrieval system, without permission in writing from the publisher.

The essay, "Sacrifice and Will," first appeared in PARABOLA, *The Magazine of Myth and Tradition,* Vol. III, No.2 (Summer 1978), pp.66–69.

Book design by Suzanne Ketchoyian

Library of Congress Catalog Card Number 93-080276

ISBN 0-9639100-0-0

CONTENTS

Introduction	i
The Ideas of George Ivanovitch Gurdjieff	1
Impressions as Food	21
In the Universe There Is No Independent Movement	27
Man Is What His Attention Is	31
The Source of Attention	35
Suffering and Attention	41
Sacrifice and Will	47
Inner Silence	55
What Is Prayer?	61
Work: The Inner Dimension	67
Letters to His Pupils	73

Acknowledgment

The editors warmly thank Alice Brazda for her diligence in transcribing Christopher Fremantle's talks and carefully preserving them; Anne Fremantle and Adam, Richard, and Hugh Fremantle for their kind permission to publish this material; Roger Lipsey for invaluable and sympathetic guidance in preparing the manuscript; Peter Nevard for his unflagging commitment; and the pupils who so generously shared with us the letters they had received.

INTRODUCTION

Of the many pupils who gathered around G. I. Gurdjieff, Christopher Fremantle was among those who continued to work for a lifetime. Tall, patrician, and soft spoken, he personified the gentleman and was able by his efforts and perhaps also by his nature to embody the ideas he transmitted.

He left a distinct mark in turn on his own pupils.

They listened to what he said, of course. Yet often it was just by watching him, trying to tune themselves to him, that they understood, at least for the moment, the seriousness of what he was trying to impart. Occasionally they shared in his joyfulness, which was apparent always, just below the surface.

He was born December 17, 1906; the youngest of five children. According to his wife, Anne, Christopher's parents were devout Episcopalians. They held family prayers every morning in which servants and guests participated. Daily Bible readings for the children were supervised by his mother.

A formative influence was his housemaster at Eton who told the boys, "be nicer," instead of scolding them. After receiving a degree from Oxford, Fremantle studied at the Royal College of Art and became a painter.

Christopher's eldest brother was killed in World War I. His lifetime pacifism stemmed from an awareness of his parents' agony in the ten days during which they watched their eldest son die from his wounds.

He met Anne Jackson in 1927, and they were married in 1930. In 1935, they were brought to the group of P. D. Ouspensky in London, and found a resonance there to their inner search. During the London blitz, Fremantle went to live with the Ouspenskys at Lyne Place, while commuting daily to his war job in London. The Fremantles were instrumental in bringing the Ouspenskys to the United States, and they worked with them in Mendham, N. J., until Ouspensky's death in 1947.

Ouspensky's widow then revealed a shocking secret: Gurdjieff was still alive. "Hurry, don't waste a moment. Go to George Ivanovitch." It was the first inkling Fremantle had that the mysterious figure who had been Ouspensky's teacher was still alive. He left at once for Paris and studied with Gurdjieff until Gurdjieff's death on October 29, 1949.

In 1951, Jeanne de Salzmann, Gurdjieff's successor, sent Fremantle to Mexico to take charge of the groups, a responsibility he carried for almost thirty years, spending every summer there and making numerous week-long visits during the year.

He returned to Paris in 1962 to work with Madame de Salzmann and stayed until 1966, when he was sent to the United States to help guide the groups in New York, Chicago, and other cities, a task he continued until his death on December 19, 1978. His grave is in Swanbourne, Buckinghamshire, England.

Fremantle's pupils ranged from beginners to older pupils responsible for transmitting the ideas of Gurdjieff. They wrote to him: What is inner work? What form should it take in the ever-changing circumstances of their lives? Some of these letters are included here.

In the 1970's, when Madame de Salzmann asked some of the older people who had worked with Gurdjieff to write about the work, Fremantle began to dictate notes on the aspects he had explored. Read aloud at meetings of his groups, these notes are reproduced in this volume.

He never gave advice on personal matters. "One can do so only if one knows all the circumstances," he said, "and of course that is impossible." He had another reason as well: his wish that his pupils deepen their own understanding without becoming dependent on him as a "guru." He had a great distaste for people's tendency to use others, to enslave them, and to take the role of "master" when life offers so many willing slaves. "We were not given this teaching to feather our nest," he said. He refused anything that might favor him personally, even a small thing like a ride home on a winter night—particularly if he felt that the one who offered was identified with the outcome of the offer.

His special study was painting. We were encouraged to work with him once a week in a study called "form and color." Professional artists and amateurs alike, we worked for six or seven hours at a time, usually in complete silence, under his tutelage. Like the Zen painters he often spoke of, we tried to practice our art by feeling the life in the subjects we gazed upon, then putting it on paper as simply and directly as possible. More than a study of painting, this was a study of seeing. We had many exercises of looking at objects, then turning away from them to record only what we had taken in. Any invention, any "filling in" with details not actually seen, was quickly apparent. We came to distinguish between the uniqueness of each object and the stereotypical appearance the mind ascribed to it. Each apple, chair or table—any object—given this form of directed attention revealed itself as quite distinctly unique, a subtle relationship of convex and concave shapes. No inanimate object was seen to be completely devoid of movement, no matter how slow. We saw the "livingness" even of rocks. Under Fremantle's patient direction, we discovered that there were no smooth lines in what we saw. Even a perfectly round orange was revealed as a complex kingdom of curves and whorls.

When the search centered on the nature of color, form was temporarily banished. We studied the tones and tints of just one color. All the tensions, struggles and clashes of color could be understood by limiting the palette to just one. The feeling evoked in us by the shades of just one were surprisingly stronger than feelings evoked by several colors together. The closer the tones, the stronger the feeling evoked. After a year, he allowed a second color to be used. By then, we understood something of the power that a color contained.

Fremantle hated pretentiousness and never mistook apparent seriousness for real effort. One day during a break in our long, silent art project, as we watched the coffee being set out and the milk and sugar passed by some pupils with a certain false solemnity, Fremantle suddenly exclaimed:

"You know of course about the famous Zen Tea Ceremony. Well, what is it? It is really just people performing the very simple daily activity of brewing and drinking tea. What makes it extraordinary is that they do it in a special way, with attention. If we could drink our coffee with attention, people would come from all over the world to watch us. Maybe they would call it the Coffee Ceremony," he added, laughing.

He showed us in many practical ways that the possibility of inner development lay in a more unified attention. When the attention is concentrated in a special way through exercises, efforts or prayer, it connects our diverse selves to create a new state in which one may experience a meeting between one's subjectivity and objective reality. This meeting brings a freedom not previously known.

For some of us, Fremantle's most frustrating and incomprehensible assertion was that conscious forces were trying to assist us, and indeed anyone who made efforts. He steadfastly refused to elaborate, and though we could not understand, we could not forget.

Once, as he was walking east on 78th Street, one of his pupils described a serious problem. "People don't realize that when they work, conscious forces come to their aid." The pupil heard an undeniable inner agreement and also a great protest. What are conscious forces? How can they possibly help me? Turning toward his pupil, he continued: "conscious forces are trying to help you. You are not alone."

Lillian Firestone Boal

"Life calls man to action, and to act he must first be."

THE IDEAS OF
GEORGE IVANOVITCH GURDJIEFF

G. I. Gurdjieff's work of teaching and writing had been almost completed when the first atomic explosion shook the world, announcing a new era; the impact of the "drug culture" on established concepts of man's consciousness and his reality was still a decade away. Yet the posthumous publication of Gurdjieff's own works, and those of P. D. Ouspensky and others dealing with his ideas, has revealed his thought as more closely related to the era which has dawned since his death than to his own.

The search which he pursued concerning questions of man's consciousness, obligations, responsibility and values and his expression, in fundamental ideas, of the unity of all that exists, seems prophetically oriented toward the present generation. The impact of his ideas is clearly visible in increasing diffusion of, and familiarity with, his thought, which flowing springlike from a pure source, sparkled with ideas, glimpses of truth, logic, paradox and apparent contradiction.

I

In his work *All and Everything,* Gurdjieff describes man as a "two-natured being." What did he intend by this? Is Gurdjieff referring to man's polarization between a lower, antecedent, and a higher, becoming, state of evolution? Or is he writing of man's participation in the fundamental duality of vibration and matter seen reflected in man as "doing" and "being"?

Life calls man to action, and to act he must first be. Just as there is a scale of action from the mere automatic reflex to the most sophisticated complex of actions, so too there is a scale of being, from the mere existence of automatically reacting man to the inner freedom, perfected reason and will of the fully realized being. Here an inescapable paradox appears.

On one side, man is a prototype of the computer, programmed by education and environment to respond to all life's diverse demands; on the other side man is a free individual, valuing his freedom and possessed of reason and free will, able to act independently of all outside influences.

Long before the computer era, Gurdjieff had diagnosed man as "a machine which has the possibility to cease being a machine."[1] To underscore this direction he proposed dividing man into "essence" and "personality" — that is, what he is at birth, and what he acquires after birth. He expressed this as "what is his own, and what is not his own."

---

[1] P.D. Ouspensky, *In Search of the Miraculous*. Harcourt, Brace & World, New York, 1949.

Today "personality" might perhaps be better described as man's conditioning, and his "essence" as his underlying individuality. Can man's personality be no more than a mirror of the influences by which he has been surrounded since birth? Yes and no, for the whole edifice of personality is built on the foundation of essence and, in some way at least, corresponds to it and is rooted in it.

Personality is composed, Gurdjieff pointed out, of a multitude of different "I"s, each one corresponding to a particular aspect of a person's life — his family, business and leisure interests; his social and political leanings; his attitude toward health, money, sex; and so on. These "I"s, in turn, become active or subside in response to outer stimuli. Each in turn dominates him; some are in conflict, some in harmony, some strangers who never meet. Man's name is legion.[2]

Such is the being of the ordinary person and the state from which all his actions arise. This state explains the complexity and chaos of his life, of the human situation, and of the world of events reflected in the media. Mankind's outer chaos is more than a reflection of his inner state of being; it is self-perpetuating. Is it possible, one may well ask, for an individual to evolve and to escape, transcending his conditioning?

---

2 New Testament, Mark 5:90.

The paradox of our inner need for freedom and our continuing inner slavery and chaos has provoked all kinds of explanations throughout the ages. Gurdjieff, in his writing, also offered symbolic reasons; but in conversation he simply stated that Nature develops man to a certain point and leaves him there, free to develop by his own effort and will, but not compelled to do so.

Were he compelled to inner growth he would once more be an automaton, and although conscious, would still be a slave moved by influences alien to himself. Development through his own free decision and efforts leads to the New Man[3] — the man of reason and knowledge, conscious and free.

Mankind and individual man, alike in process of evolution, exhibit at times both the characteristics of the animal kingdom and those of the man yet to become. But the man who will appear is far from what, in our myopic vision, we see as our becoming; at those rare moments of greatly heightened experience, which occur in the life of the majority of men, the new state appears as both unexpected and familiar, and by no means a linear projection of habitual states. On the contrary, at such moments it is as though man has entered a new dimension in himself.

[3] New Testament, Ephesians 4:24; Colossians 3:10.

The automaton, set in motion by reaction to outside influences, is still present in these moments; but the active germ of a New Man, motivated by the voice of conscience, remains free to coexist with and complement the automaton. The automatic and conscious natures together form a coherent unity, larger than their sum, which includes their duality without being divided by it.

Such a view, born of transient moments of a new vision, may lead to a further concept, presented in open or hidden form in almost all the great religious traditions. When purely mechanical man dies, there is no inner stable formation in him capable of surviving and continuing to manifest his individuality. The elements of his inner life — his mind, thought and feeling, and his highest intellect and emotion — are without adequate substance to survive the death of the physical body. There has not been formed, in his lifetime, an "astral" body — that is, an inner body composed of fine materials and corresponding to the psychic functions of thought and feeling.

The full manifestation of man's dual nature requires, Gurdjieff proposed, the gradual crystallization during his lifetime of an inner "astral" body, stable and corresponding to an evolved psyche. This psyche, which has its own structure and order, is capable of obeying the inner authority, the voice of truth known through the conscious, evolved reason and conscience.

This new crystallization, or "higher being body," is the vehicle which, immortal relative to the earthly body, will continue to live and manifest in its own proper sphere after the death of the physical body. This "astral" body may in its turn become the basis of a new and yet finer crystallization, the supreme being body, immortal in the full sense of the word.

II

"Your principal mistake," Gurdjieff said in an early talk with Ouspensky, "consists in thinking that you always have consciousness. In reality consciousness is a property which is continually changing. Now it is present, now it is not present. And there are different degrees and levels of consciousness....We have only the possibility of consciousness and rare flashes of it."

Gurdjieff divided consciousness into four levels: "sleep," "waking," the "self-conscious" state and "objective consciousness"—that is, a fully awakened state. Ordinary man lives only in the first two and may be compared, he said, to a man living in a richly furnished house who lives in only two rooms in the basement. These two rooms are sleep and the waking state in which we spend our lives, make war, commit crimes, and try to solve the problems for which this state itself is responsible. The real awakening is experienced in the upper rooms, the third and fourth states of consciousness.

Each level or state of consciousness is experienced according to the degree of inner connectedness at the time of the experience. All the psychic equipment necessary for experiencing full consciousness already exists in every man, but some or all of the connections necessary are missing. The degree of consciousness depends on the quality of the brain system a being possesses and on its coherence or connectedness.

Objectively speaking, Gurdjieff insisted, man has not one but several brains, each corresponding to and controlling a definite function: thought, emotion, motor, instinctive and sex functions, each possessing its own separate and distinct intelligence that governs its action. What present-day scientific thought calls the "subconscious," Gurdjieff regarded as composed partly of the action, outside the general awareness, of the five mentioned functions, and partly of the action of the two higher faculties — higher emotional and higher intellectual — which, on account of their speed and breadth of vision, lie beyond the general awareness.

These two higher faculties, or centers, are responsible for the third and fourth states of consciousness, called by Gurdjieff "self-consciousness" and "objective consciousness," and for psychic phenomena which extend far beyond the ordinary. These states, recognized in all the great religious traditions, are referred to in the West by such names as "illumination," "cosmic consciousness," "union" and "ecstasy," and in the East by such names as "nirvana," "samadhi," "satori," and so on. Such experiences can only be fleetingly experienced and partially remembered by ordinary thought because their speed and universality is beyond the range of its operation, words and concepts.

Throughout the centuries experiences with drugs have also been associated with supernormal states of consciousness, and modern developments in biochemistry have thrown light on the material or chemical aspects of different drug-induced states. The fact that they are artificially induced and not voluntary — that is, not organic and integral — makes them useless for acquiring exact knowledge or control of the transition from one state of consciousness to another.

Gurdjieff's structured idea, comprising the four above-mentioned states of consciousness and five functional centers — those of thought, emotion, movement, instinct and sex — with two higher functions beyond the range of normal awareness, provides a framework which allows the whole range of human experience, in all its complexity, to be connected together in an orderly whole. Without such a framework, effective self-study proves almost impossible. Even with its help, self-observation is inevitably subjective and needs careful verification in group or "school" conditions to eliminate the risk of fantasy and to achieve objectivity.

For Gurdjieff, experience of the above four states of consciousness and their variations depends on the degree of inner connectedness between the brains or centers controlling the functions. Deep sleep he regarded as a state in which each center, while continuing to function independently, is entirely dissociated from all the others. The ascending degrees of awareness, from automatic dreams to the highest objective consciousness, are experienced in the measure of the linkage of each center with the others.

Those fine psychic materials which are able to link man's ordinary waking consciousness with the higher centers are not present in adequate quantities in normal functioning; if accidentally present they do not remain long enough to allow an ordered study of transition to higher states.

The aim of "school" methods and work includes knowledge of conditions favoring the production of these fine materials in the organism, and so of the laws governing voluntary transitions from one state of consciousness to another. Ascetic practices, periods of fasts or special observances, rituals or sacred dances, and the use of music and incense were originally connected with establishing conditions for study of the production of materials in the organism leading to intentional changes of state. While religious tradition has preserved many such ancient forms, almost all of their essential content has been lost.

Self-study is the means of acquiring a special inner attention which participates in the inner state of connectedness, and also serves for acquiring exact knowledge of conditions leading to higher states of consciousness — those in which knowledge has a universality and timelessness far beyond that of ordinary subjective knowledge. Examples exist in sacred literature, architecture, art and music which testify to these qualities and to the existence of such knowledge.

Gurdjieff emphasized that the key to changes of consciousness is in the attention. Only through correctly understood and adequately developed powers of attention can self-observation become deep enough to reveal the knowledge called, for this very reason, the "secret" doctrine. All exercises of concentration, posture or breathing, as Sri Ramana Maharshi once remarked, are for the sole purpose of gaining control of the attention; when the attention is controlled such exercises are not necessary.

In this connection, Gurdjieff — who had made a profound study of the practices of every tradition — pointed out that the wastage of fine or psychic material in the ordinary man is so great, that development of an adequate degree of attention cannot take place directly. The chaotic state of the centers results in a distracted and dispersed attention which has not the necessary power. The main causes of dispersal are associative movements of thought, conflicts and negative states in the emotions, and muscular bodily tensions, all of which consume great quantities of very fine energies unproductively.

Without prior work on such negative features, traditional ways of bringing new levels of attention, including practices connected with meditation, prayer, and physical postures or rites, cannot be expected to yield results of the desired order.

A particularly interesting aspect of Gurdjieff's ideas is that rightly directed attention is creative or catalytic; that is, it promotes the production of the specific materials necessary to fully connect the centers, and it has a crucial action in allowing impressions received through the senses (also a source of fine materials) to be absorbed on an adequate scale.

The particular forms of attention required — those in which the field of attention includes both the "outer" sense perceptions and the "inner" awareness of movements of thought, feeling and bodily energies — were known in all periods and described by such names as recollection, contemplation, *sativichare,* and so on. Gurdjieff coined a word to renew the concept of this practice in contemporary terms — "self-remembering" was the expression he used.

This controlled attention never occurs automatically and is the very antithesis of the over-involved attention characteristically found in everyday living, in which the attention is hypnotically drawn to the outer world, so that almost no inner movements are experienced and no objective knowledge of them can arise.

Unless the form of attention is changed and a special inner awareness is cultivated, exact knowledge of the inner conditions which govern voluntary changes of state is impossible. It is to create the possibility of acquiring and transmitting knowledge of this kind that esoteric schools exist.

III

For Gurdjieff the burning questions of man's spiritual development and illumination were not to be placed in the context of monastery, ashram or Himalayan cave, but in the street and the home, in the office, factory or field. The recluse's life is a vocation for the few; the call to interior growth is to all men and especially to the good householder.

From his first meeting with Ouspensky, already a well-known thinker, writer and lecturer, his conversations dealt with fundamental questions of the unity of all creation, consciousness and the significance of man's life on the earth — themes of Ouspensky's published works. These conversations so impressed Ouspensky that he later noted: "In his explanations I felt the assurance of a specialist, a very fine analysis of facts, and a *system* which I could not grasp...."[4] It was as though the outline of a majestic building had been drawn but the details of the facade were not yet clearly visible.

Gurdjieff spoke with him of the Great Knowledge as the knowledge of the unity of the laws through which the creation of all the worlds takes place. Starting from the Hermetic principle, *As above, so below,* he explained the first great cosmic law of tri-

---

[4] Ouspensky, *In Search*, ch. 1.

unity, of three principles: action, resistance and equilibrium, and showed its action in the creation of the worlds of the cosmos and its parallel action in the interior world of man.

The Creative Will resounds from the Absolute as pure vibration — God the Word. As these vibrations extend and diminish in space, their material aspect becomes denser. At certain lawful points of condensation of vibration and matter, the infinite world of galaxies, suns and planetary systems with their satellites arise. The current of creation, emanating from the Absolute, the infinite All, flows to the Void, the infinite Nothing, and thence returns to its source.

This process, called into being by the Will of the Absolute, and maintained at every step by the Law of Tri-unity, or trinity of forces, creates the phenomena of the worlds and in so doing obeys the second great cosmic law, the Law of Seven or of octaves. The action of this law, parallel with the musical scale, manifests seven "notes" or steps and two "intervals" or points of retardation of vibration. For an octave to continue to completion, forces coming from without must intervene in these intervals. The seven notes are the points of condensation of matter and vibration at which the worlds come into being; thus the whole of creation, from the Absolute to the Void, forms a complete octave.

The intervals in this cosmic octave correspond to the place of the semitones in the musical scale: between *do* and *si*, and between *fa* and *mi*. That is, between the Absolute and all the Worlds, and between the planets and the earth. In the latter interval man, as a part of organic life on the earth, plays a vital role in the cosmic process.

In this way the ray of creation passes from unity to diversity, following an order established by these two laws. The line of action of the octave, like the trunk of a tree branching out, gives rise to secondary octaves; these in their turn give rise to third-order octaves, forming twigs on the branches. Anyone, said Gurdjieff, who completely understands the Law of Tri-unity and the Law of Seven has the key to the understanding of unity, because he will understand the origin of every phenomenon, its place and its results.

As above, so below. Above, the macrocosmos is the universe; below, created by the same laws operating on another level, the microcosmos is man, a perfect reflection of it in its structure and laws. But only complete man, fully realized, is so related. He alone is destined and is able, by his qualities of will, freedom and pure reason, to play a cosmic role (like the angels and archangels of tradition) in governing and maintaining the created worlds. By nature a receiver and transmitter, the complete man receives from the highest spheres of creation and transmits to the earth and to humanity. Mechanical man, the "sleeping" man whom we know, is the seed whose possibilities are latent and whose germination depends on himself. Like the source from which he issues, his nature is sacred and essentially free. He may realize his possibilities or die unrealized. Nothing is imposed on him by nature, and his growth, if it occurs, will include the development of individuality and real Will.

In man himself, a universe in miniature, the same laws of trinity and of the octave operate. Thus the body chemistry develops metabolically by steps the three types of raw materials of food, air and impressions to produce the subtle materials which energize the thought, feelings and body. The food he eats is digested and, in metabolizing, obeys the Law of Octaves. In the first interval where outside help is required, air enters the body, purifying the blood and assisting the food process to develop further to the point where another interval occurs and a shock is necessary. There the third food, the impressions received through the senses, is not digested adequately, and without conscious effort the impressions do not provide the psychic fuels necessary for complete awakening.

Automatically the octave of food reaches the highest levels of material required for the maintenance and reproduction of the bodily organism. Without the intervention of the will, the octave of the second food, air drawn into the lungs, will not achieve the awakening of the higher faculties it was designed to nourish. This voluntary action in the form of a conscious shock allows the development of substances derived from the air to proceed further, and by this action man awakes. For a total awakening man needs more subtle fuels derived from the continued digestion of impressions. For higher thought and feeling to appear, a second conscious shock is required, touching the emotional life.

These two conscious efforts, necessary for man's awakening, Gurdjieff referred to as "conscious labor and intentional suffering."

The first awakening of man is to his nullity, multiplicity and inner chaos. It may create in him a need to crystallize, through conscious work on himself, an inner order—that is, to bring about conditions within himself favorable to the growth of consciousness and of an awakened psyche capable of self-knowledge, understanding and true reason. The first crystallization of an inner order, resulting from long and correct work on himself, is the crystallization of the astral body within the physical body. This is the New Man, whose life is immortal in relation to the physical body. The astral body, when formed, can become the means of crystallizing a still more subtle body, the higher being-body, built from materials developed by conscious inner work. The higher body, endowed with pure reason, is immortal in relation to the astral body. Only the highest being-body is truly immortal.

For Gurdjieff such ideas were the direct expression of universal laws, and their sense was to awaken in those who could hear, an urgent awareness of man's need to live in the world in terms of his deeper nature, essential individuality and will. For man, compelled to serve Great Nature, the highest service is by virtue of being, conscience, pure reason and will. But due to the results of contemporary education and the environment in which he lives, it is usually only in moments of great shock or deep disillusionment that man awakes and is able to hear the voice of conscience.

In order, Gurdjieff said, to awaken a conscience capable of participating in every action, a personal aim is needed and correct methods. It is for this awakening and realization, necessary for mankind, that Schools exist.

Gurdjieff defined as follows the five strivings needed for the awakening of conscience[5]:

---

[5] G.I. Gurdjieff, *Beelzebub's Tales to His Grandson: An Objectively Impartial Criticism of the Life of Man.* E.P. Dutton & Company, Inc., New York, 1964, ch. 27.

"The first striving: to have in their ordinary being existence everything satisfying and really necessary for their planetary body.

"The second striving: to have a constant and unflagging instinctive need for self-perfection in the sense of being.

"The third: the conscious striving to know ever more and more concerning the laws of World-creation and World-maintenance.

"The fourth: the striving from the beginning of their existence to pay for their arising and their individuality as quickly as possible, in order afterwards to be free to lighten as much as possible the Sorrow of our COMMON FATHER..

"And the fifth: the striving always to assist the most rapid perfecting of other beings, both those similar to oneself and those of other forms, up to the degree of the sacred 'Martfotai' that is up to the degree of self-individuality."

"Is there another mode of receiving impressions which can feed the psyche rather than merely produce movement of an automatic kind?"

IMPRESSIONS AS FOOD

What is life?

From the neutron to the galaxies, every form of life has its birth, its span and its period of decay. Life is everywhere. In different spheres its form obeys different laws.

Organic life as it exists on earth in every form — vegetable, animal or human — is maintained by the same principles: by food intake and elimination of waste and by programmed response to stimuli. It is in this last respect that the question of impressions is important, for while they appear basically to be connected with the preservation of life in man, they can also be looked at as food.

Impressions are sense-contacts — in reality, contacts between electromagnetic forces or fields. These contacts serve as stimuli; the life in which they occur responds either in accordance with nature's programming (for preserving and continuing the species) or through the exercise of an independent intelligence.

Even very primitive forms of life accept some materials and reject others in maintaining their lifecycle, by mysterious processes only now beginning to be understood. In plant life, programming and intelligence still seem indistinguishable. In man, responses are on so many levels that, although instinct and intelligence seem separate, a line dividing the two cannot be defined.

The belief in free will arises because conscious intelligence and nature's programming seem to have been developed in man such that each can act independently of, or contrary to, the other. The separation of programming and intelligence leads to a convenient, if arbitrary, distinction between the body and the psyche.

The basic support of the body is what man eats and the air he breathes. The support of his psyche is in the impressions received through the senses, or from within. For example, sense-impressions give rise to the possibility of associative thought, conceptual knowledge and emotional responses of a quality beyond that of the instinctive. Development of evolving individuals, and a corresponding culture, can be related to evolution through the quality of impressions received by the psyche.

Development of scientific and technological instrumentation, for example, serves to enhance and allow effective analysis of otherwise imperceptible impressions. Modern civilization, from the conquest of space to the conquest of disease, arises from this enhancement of sense-impressions, bringing new material for the psychic function, realized as new levels of knowledge.

The study of impressions as a food, nourishing the psyche and developing new levels of its functioning, seems inevitable. However, it involves turning away from pure technology toward the great traditions that affirm that man's psyche has been planned by nature for an extraordinary degree of evolution in a dimension quite different from that in which technology has led.

The question may be stated in another way. While scientific perfection makes available a far wider range of impressions, man's receptive apparatus has not been correspondingly improved. Is improvement in the quality of human receptiveness possible?

What about man's absorption of impressions? Although studies have been made of the deprivation of impressions and its effect, of the action of suggestion and of hypnosis, for example, another equally important side has been neglected. This is the phenomenon of inattention. When music is heard, a book read, or a conversation is in progress, the stream of impressions provokes continual associations; these tend to absorb the attention, creating gaps in the stream of conscious reception.

The reality of the world is thus received through a screen of reactions, comments and judgments. This is so continuous that often it is hardly noticed. How much of our reality is the construction from materials recorded in the memory by associative thought and feeling? It is the way we view the situation at the moment of action which is decisive, rather than the reality existing in the moment. If the view and the reality agree, all is well; but if they diverge, then trouble ensues. Man's constant delusion is that each person is aware of reality around him.

For progress toward a new dimension of experience, a study of the mechanism of perception is necessary, as well as a closer appraisal of the nature of our perception of truth.

"...the force of attention emanates from life itself and again returns to life as a creative and regenerative force."

IN THE UNIVERSE THERE IS NO INDEPENDENT MOVEMENT

In the universe as we know it there is no independent movement. The whole life of the universe is maintained by interaction of one body with another from the subatomic to the galactic, according to law. The forms of life are maintained from birth through maturity to death and decay by exchange of energies, whether on the scale of the viral or the stellar.

Man is the slave of this universal movement. Can there be in man any independent energy or any independent movement?

Individually man has always had the illusion that he is free, but this freedom is not his. He is oppressed by the forces that surround him: economic, social and political, and by those within him such as the need for food, shelter and continuation of the species. In all this which compels and impels man from the time he is born until he dies, it is difficult to find anything but the gigantic automatism of Mother Nature. It is only when we take into account the ancient idea attributed to Hermes Trismegistus that man the microcosm is a reflection of the universal macrocosm, that we find an opening toward the question: Are there in man not only energies belonging to the exchange by which his life is supported, but also energies of a higher order related to life of another level where a relative state of freedom exists?

In *In Search of the Miraculous*, P.D. Ouspensky describes a diagram given by G.I. Gurdjieff, in which life in the universe ascends by steps of three related forms of life on a ladder of creation from mineral to the Most Holy. Here man is seen as the highest element in the vertebrate triad and the lowest in the succeeding angelic triad. This diagram Gurdjieff called the "Diagram of Everything Living."

On the scale of the universe, there can be nothing fully independent in man. Seen from the ascending movement, he is the slave of the forces of heredity and environment, obeying the laws of evolution. Approached from above from unity in diversity, he shares in the independence of this creation to a relative degree.

If we examine our own experience, we are bound to conclude that the areas in which man's inborn creative freedom appears are principally those of thought and feeling. The existence in sacred literature and art of a thought and an emotion able to span centuries with its truth seems to support this finding.

There seems to be a possibility of establishing by empirical method that evolution in man is evolution toward freedom, toward universality of thought and feeling and toward universality of truth. Freedom thus comes to be seen as a dynamic situation rather than a static aspect of man's life.

We are bound to conclude that the freedom which man so earnestly seeks is a freedom of movement of his inner energies, liberated from the mechanical forces of his environment and transformed within him toward a universal truth.

Unless the study of energy is oriented toward consciousness, it becomes an endless academic study unredeemed by any revelation of energy as the bearer of life.

"It seems impossible to find a point where attention can be separated from life itself..."

MAN IS WHAT HIS ATTENTION IS

In his ordinary way of being, man's attention is dispersed in responding to the many demands of life. G.I. Gurdjieff brought back into currency the idea that attention is the most powerful creative force in man.

The lawyer, the artist or the businessman may be aware of this. They experience that a certain degree of attention concentrated on a problem enables them to reach areas of the mind or feelings from which new ideas arise. At such moments it is certain that the degree of attention has played a vital role.

This turning of the attention to search for new levels of thought and feeling within is highly significant. But it must be noted that introversion alone does not act in this way. There must be an attention directed simultaneously to the outer and inner world. Creation is a two-way street. As Picasso remarked, "You must breathe in *and* breathe out."

In the religious traditions this turning of the attention is present. Concentration in prayer of the Judaeo-Christian, the Pratiyahara of Yoga, the Vichara of the Hindu and the Zen Koan are the means for reaching enlightenment.

What is the action of attention when directed inward?

It seems to be generally accepted that where a man is faced with great danger or is inspired by great love, the hero appears in him: a keener awareness, overwhelming feeling, physical and moral strength of an extraordinary kind. Are these changes of his psychic state due to a total focus on the object of danger or of love? Is it attention that unites all his faculties of thought, feeling and body in a common aim?

Perhaps it is in the power of creating unity that attention acts as a creative force. The man in deep meditation feels, if we are to believe the most authentic descriptions, not only his own unity, but a transcendent unity - that of all men, of all truth.

In this case also, man is what his attention is.

"...active attention is not continuous, it consists of moments of voluntary renewal. One may say, 'now I will have an active attention resting on such and such a thing,' but at every moment it has to be renewed; and it is renewed by one's wish, or by one's will."

THE SOURCE OF ATTENTION

The source of attention, our means of contact and communication through the senses, is very close to the mystery of life. Attention, like a magnet, draws impressions to us from without and within, connecting us to the world around and protecting us from it.

In accordance with the received impressions, we respond just as a cell responds to its environment, a plant seeks the light or an animal is alerted to danger; so each living being automatically responds to outer stimuli.

Can a line be drawn between chemical reactions in the cell and conscious action in man? Does the reign of chemistry at a certain point give place to the reign of consciousness?

Attention in man appears to differ from that of the lower forms of life in that it can be either automatic or conscious. The question arises: is it his capacity for conscious attention which demarcates man from the animal kingdom?

In man, quality of attention is reflected in the quality of his knowledge. When the attention is automatic, the impressions received are fragmentary and indistinct; when it is conscious, they are sharp and vivid. If the attention is wholly occupied elsewhere, impressions are scarcely received.

If a man sets out from home in the morning, for example, and his thoughts are involved with the coming day, he hardly sees the familiar trees and houses. But if the sun is shining and the air is brilliant and his attention is strongly called to the present moment, he may be filled with a sudden wonder. The whole scene appears sharply delineated and is deeply imprinted on his memory.

Even though he would like to stop right there and reflect on the scene in that vivid awareness, the pressures of life crowd in on him, and he seems fated to be called away and pass his day without enjoying this conscious state of presence again.

For example, waking up in a strange room, for a moment I may not know where I am. My attention is caught by my perceptions, but associations have not begun to operate; I have awakened to a strange world. The next moment the associations in my memory begin to work; I recognize the room, then I remember coming here and events of the previous day which brought me here. My attention is no longer in the present alone, it is also in my associations. Moments later the alarm clock sounds. It too calls my attention and gives a shock. A new train of associations instantly begins. The perception of the sound recalls how I had set it to wake me at that time because I have things to do. My thought switches from the past to the future and again the present moment disappears from view as my attention is carried away once more by the flow of associations.

As I begin to dress almost automatically, attention becomes more and more dispersed; many associations are competing in the increasing flow of thought about the day ahead. I am no more than minimally aware of the room where I am until the phone rings and recalls me to my surroundings. I lift the receiver and a friend is speaking about a problem and questioning me. The associations respond to a new shock and move smoothly and coherently in a different direction, and again the room and my surroundings merge into the background.

Before the day begins I would like to be quiet for a moment and collect myself, but the water is boiling for my coffee and the time is short. I make the coffee, pour myself some and take the first sip, and again new associations carry me away.

What does it all mean?

Is this a destiny imposed on man? Is the very essence of the human situation man's freedom to escape from this domination and his inability to do so?

My attention, this power tool for communication, is not mine. It remains almost entirely at the disposal of life's imperative needs or whatever event comes along and forces an impression on my senses and my mind. Yet it is mine; it springs from me, from my life; it is a part of my life force which ceases to be mine in so far as it does not obey my conscious being but is constantly enslaved by the outside world.

Is this paradox my fate, our fate, the human situation? Could this attention be the means of living in conscious communication with myself and the world around me as it changes from moment to moment? Am I condemned to live as a prisoner of my conditioning and my automatic associations?

I have tried to understand this phenomenon by observing animals and birds in the wild. They too have attention, an alertness for possible danger. Their ears, eyes and senses are ceaselessly on guard; at a movement, a sound, they freeze. If it is danger, their reaction is instantaneous; if it proves something familiar, they continue what they were doing.

Is the security mechanism, and the associations connected with it, at the root of our own over-involvement in the outside world? Is the process of evolution connected with the liberation of the attention an abandonment of a search for security as the animal knows it?

Insofar as I am not in immediate danger, do I need to obey the automatic dispersal of attention continually directed outward, taken first by one thing and then by another, like that of an animal? If the psyche is freed from fear, and the attention liberated for conscious direction, will it naturally develop to new levels? I see that when my attention is controlled through an active wish it links me continuously with the faculties of my psyche. I can think better, feel more sensitively and perceive more sharply.

Is there a vital synthesis at work in which a new force arising from the interplay of attention and consciousness links me to a timeless world? Why is it that at these moments there is a sense of recognition as well as of mystery? And the world, so different from the one I was in a few moments before, now fills me with questioning.

Are these moments, isolated by long periods of time, moments in which everything is lucid, full of implications, of emotions, the indication of the presence of a new world of thought and feeling corresponding to an evolved mankind?

"...choice seems to exist on every level, and at each point where the possibility of attention appears, the possibility of choice appears."

SUFFERING AND ATTENTION

How is the utilization of suffering possible? Is man's will stronger than nature?

Strong impressions attract our attention. This is an integral factor in the programming of nature for the preservation and continuance of our life.

The impressions received are in three categories: those that favor; those that are neutral; and those that threaten. The programmed response to the first category is in terms of joy or pleasure; to the second, indifference; to the third, resistance to or avoidance of suffering and danger. The impressions which threaten life and well-being are felt as suffering or pain and create strong reactions in the body and psyche corresponding to the need for security.

Pain or its threat releases potent and subtle materials which the chemistry of the body needs for survival — for speed or strength, for battle or endurance. These responses affect the chemistry both of the body and of the psyche and are accompanied by courage or fear, anger or violence, elation or depression. The arousing of these emotions and the chemical changes accompanying them connect directly or indirectly with strong impressions, and they absorb a great deal of energy.

Since the amount of energy available to man's organism is limited by his daily intake of food and air, his inner development and the manifestation of new states of consciousness depend on the economical utilization of these materials. The impressions which warn the body of danger, like those which give the senses pleasure, need to be used economically and constructively. Instead of expressing or rejecting reactions to strong impressions, they can be transformed in man; hence the scriptural saying: "The stone which the builders rejected, the same is become the head of the corner: this is the Lord's doing, and it is marvellous in our eyes."[6]

Nature, it must be believed, has programmed man not only for survival but also for the possibility of evolution. In giving man the power to direct his attention voluntarily, Nature has given him the germ of free will. The testimony of the great prophets is unanimous and their lives bear witness to this. Were evolution to occur mechanically, there would not be development of consciousness and freedom — qualities which separate the human from the animal.

The attention, automatically attracted to every strong impression, goes out to the object producing the impression in such a way that the energy of the attention is caught, absorbed in the reaction, and lost.

[6] New Testament, Matthew 21:42.

But with an attention consciously controlled, Gurdjieff maintained, a different evolutionary process is set in motion.

Suffering is the inevitable complement of life, even when life itself is not in question. Suffering brings discomfort, misery or self-pity. Can we observe in ourselves how the substances of this suffering may be integrated in the psyche to bring, not violence, but new levels of consciousness and positive states such as love, compassion and joy?

According to Gurdjieff's ideas, all impressions received are food for the psyche, but only a minute proportion of those reaching us penetrate deeply enough to serve this purpose. Here the power to direct attention is crucial. By conscious attention the impressions are assimilated.

Gurdjieff looked on conscious attention as a catalyst. Automatic attention provides man with security; but conscious attention, or more precisely, an awareness, an attention that simultaneously includes both man's outer and inner world, is the key to evolution. Its dual function is outward survival and inner creation.

Gurdjieff proposed, and invited practical verification, that this inner attention catalyzes a further development of fine substances feeding the psychic mechanisms and allows an opening toward a more universal level of thought and feeling.

This point of view can, he claimed, be studied and verified through practices of self-observation or recollection.

Self-observation reveals that, where there is conscious attention, the products of suffering are not obliged to flow into the channels of the defense mechanisms, since in most of the situations producing suffering, life and well-being are not at stake. When, through the practice of recollected attention, this movement toward defense becomes familiar, it is possible for the feelings to redirect it in such a way as to effect its transformation into positive feelings. Although these substances are too fine for present techniques of analysis, the nature of this action of conscious attention can be experienced and verified.

This transformation demands, first of all, the establishment of an inner order. Where inner chaos prevails, the creative action of such an inner work may only add force to disorder. As in the ascent of Mount Analogue, it is better to make the ascent in company with an experienced guide.[7]

---

[7] René Daumal, *Mount Analogue: An Authentic Narrative*. Vincent Stuart Publishers Ltd., London, 1959, p. 38.

"The automatic state dominates, because of the absence of voluntary attention. There is a certain amount of energy available for voluntary attention, which is too small to study the process of will. Many acts of voluntary attention produce accumulation of force. Perhaps will must be seen as a state rather than an act."

SACRIFICE AND WILL

The idea of sacrifice as a "making sacred" has always been very much a part of western thought. Today the word remains, but it is more often used in the political and economic sense of belt-tightening or of accepting inconveniences necessary for the common welfare, or even as a sort of tradeoff or exchange. There is no other word to carry its primal meaning; so it is necessary to restore the word to its original significance and bring it back to currency, for it is not only a word but a dynamic idea, as alive now as ever, although seemingly out-of-date. And it is also a paradox.

If, as tradition says, the universe is created, then everything must be sacred, because this quality derives from the Creator; so the idea of "making sacred" is redundant. But if in accord with some present-day thought, our universe is accidental, arising from an unknown beginning, then nothing in it is or will become sacred. And our understanding of this contradiction is not helped by the traditional Christian outlook which, leaning on the words, "Greater love hath no man than this, that a man lay down his life for his friends,"[8] speaks of death as "the supreme sacrifice"; nor is it helped by traditional sacrificial rites in which the blood of victims is offered.

[8] New Testament, John 15:13.

How can the destruction of life, whether on the altar or the battlefield, render life itself sacred?

I think the reconciling element between these conflicting aspects of meaning must be looked for in the view of sacrifice as an essential part of the life process, rather than as an isolated act of expiation. There is a striking, though very brief, passage in the Gospel of St. John in which Christ says (apparently referring to the Eleusinian mysteries, since Philip had just announced that two Greeks wished to speak with him): "Except a corn of wheat fall into the ground and die, it abideth alone, but if it die it bringeth forth much fruit." In this statement, and in the context of the Greek mysteries, the idea of sacrifice and death is linked together with that of rebirth and fulfillment. That is, the idea of sacrifice is linked with that of immortality, life beyond time; "before Abraham was, I am." In joining sacrifice, suffering and death with the concept of transformation and of the continuity of life as a total process, all the apparent contradictions are resolved. The perspective that life itself does not die, but is expressed in constant transformation and movement, lies at the root of major religious traditions in both East and West.

Here in the light of modern investigative thought, the question arises: what actually is the transforming action of sacrifice and suffering upon the person who offers it? The first contemporary teaching to have posed this question seems to have been that of Gurdjieff, with his emphasis on "conscious labors and intentional suffering." Every sacrifice involves suffering, sometimes beneficial and sometimes not; what seems to distinguish "useful" strengthening and transformative suffering from that which is useless and distorting is precisely its intentional quality. If the suffering is not voluntarily accepted, it turns into bitterness, as Lot's wife turned into salt.

But with the idea of voluntary sacrifice other questions arise. Today, the medieval Christian asceticism that expressed itself in self-torture seems remote; and such tendency is suspect, as masochism or at best just another ego trip. So the question becomes important: what is the nature of, and whose is the "will" behind this voluntary action? What is the transforming role of personal will in sacrifice? What, indeed, is that which we call "will"? We know so much more about "self-will," with its ego motivations, than about human will itself. How are we to separate real will from the conditioned responses and defenses formed around a person from birth?

Ramana Maharshi once commented that to gain control of the attention is the sole aim of all spiritual exercises and disciplines, thus aligning himself with Ramakrishna who, a century earlier, had followed for twelve years different disciplines of great traditional religions and concluded that they did not differ in essence. Gurdjieff, too, pointed to attention as the unique tool for acquiring objective, nonegoistic will. The attention to which they refer is certainly not that which is continually darting from one thing to the next, distracted by every happening and every association, nor that which is helplessly absorbed in some problem. Neither kind has the activity and stability capable of resisting the automatic, conditioned responses which rule our behavior. When suffering appears, these automatic impulses push us toward escape; where sacrifice is involved, toward compromise or complacency. Only an independent and stable attention can be aware of the moment of decision and choice, can detect a deviation from the decision before it gathers momentum.

Perhaps it can be said that real will is the product of intention and of the strong forces released in us by suffering. Suffering and danger free vast amounts of fine energy which have observable physical manifestations: under threat from a charging bull a man leaps obstacles he could never clear in cold blood; when a child is in danger a mother can forego sleep for days and nights because an extraordinary energy is present. But except at such moments we are not in control of these capacities and not even aware of them; they are not available to us.

All teachings regarding conscious transformation seek ways of coming into relationship with these inner powers. Traditional counsels of "action without attachment," ascetic practices of various kinds, deep meditation and contemplation, are means for reaching and studying an attention which can transform, that is, an attention which can link a man with his deepest aspiration and the power to resist the automatism of flight in the face of suffering.

Modern scientific psychology has begun to study those areas crucial to development in man's psyche, and to acquire some information about them. This direction interested the late Abraham Maslow and other researchers who have pursued it through psychological studies or through laboratory measurement of the psychological effects of meditation; but not nearly enough is yet known. In medicine, current research is reported to be revealing the part played by fine energies — subatomic particles — in the process of physiological and neurological response. Looking further ahead, particle physics will surely throw new light on the action on man's psyche of fine energies entering our world from the cosmos. When these aspects of the natural sciences reach their flowering, it may well be found that they restate, more lucidly and in contemporary terms, ancient traditional teachings concerning the true role of sacrifice. The last thirty years have brought about a rapprochement between metaphysical and scientific thought, and it seems quite possible that a new understanding, confirmed by research, will show the role of sacrifice and suffering as vital forces in the chain of life's evolution and transformation.

"...it is that elusive quality, sincerity with myself, which brings about contact with 'being'..."

INNER SILENCE

What do we really know of our experience of life?

Experiments made by the National Aeronautics and Space Administration proved that a person almost entirely deprived of external impressions finds his situation insupportable after a few hours and seems to be in danger of losing his reason. Impressions form the food necessary for the maintenance of life from moment to moment.

The impressions which arrive from the world around us fall upon the senses: sight, smell, touch and so on and, entering into the psyche, meet with the mechanisms of thought and feeling where they create an immediate response.

This response constitutes the security mechanism common to the whole animal world and probably to all organic life; the familiar is recognized, the unfamiliar gives rise to fear.

The impulse of the impression is absorbed and produces a movement in the mechanism of thought, feeling and instinct. In the thought this movement becomes a chain of associations; in the feeling it becomes like or dislike, pleasure or fear; in the instinct it produces a corresponding response of posture or action.

There are impressions which produce action, others which produce only movement of thought and feeling, still others which are stored in the subconscious without our being aware of them, and which may nevertheless produce secondary or subliminal reactions.

These movements which constitute man's automatic, conditioned response to life around him can be compared to the action of a computer which is programmed but does not possess consciousness. It cannot strictly be considered that impressions received in this way reach the intelligence of the centers. The question arises: is there another mode of receiving impressions which can feed the psyche rather than merely produce movement of an automatic kind? That is to say, can man open himself to impressions in such a way that his thought and feeling receive a constant renewal from the world in which he lives?

For this to be possible we must consider the question of what may be called "inner silence." When a man's attention is not entirely taken by associative movements and these movements are allowed to die down, he experiences inner silence.

This silence is either a passive state or one accompanied by an active attention, perhaps in the thoughtless form of a question without an answer. That is to say, all the automatic data received from the senses stored in the computer are refused consciously, and the attention is actively engaged in a state of continuing question. Such, for example, is the state of a man listening, trying to catch an almost inaudible sound as his whole body, feeling and thought are concentrated in the attempt to catch the sound. It would seem that impressions which come into this inner silence do not immediately produce a mechanized reaction which deflect them automatically. They possess an intensity, a richness, which touches both the thought and the feeling and which seems to bring a much more intimate and fruitful contact with man's outer and inner reality.

The very surprise and wonder of this unexpected richness will set off the associations in the computer, and again the mechanical state fills the psyche. But where the attention is strong enough to resist this movement, impressions continue to connect man in a way which vivifies his thought, feeling and understanding.

At the same time he becomes aware that not only are there impressions of an external kind, but that he also receives inner impressions through which he feels relationships which are imperceptible to the senses. He no longer feels isolated and separated in the way he did before. He is no longer alone.

"One always comes back at these times to the fundamental fact, which is at the base of all "observation," that "I" and "my state" are not the same."

WHAT IS PRAYER?

"...Yet the most important of all is prayer, the fourth weapon in this war...."[9]

The moment we inquire into the nature of prayer, so many questions appear that we run the risk of being stopped before starting. Yet we see three questions that may be held as the center, or core, of inquiry.

What is prayer? How could we pray? To what could we pray?

And a fourth question immediately presents itself: what is it in man that prompts him to prayer? Perhaps we could start here. Let us at the outset jettison the idea of prayer as supplication, eliminating the notion of prayer to someone for something.

It could be said at this point we see prayer as an active element, rather than a passive state of petition. A means, not for gain, an "adding to," but an active method of coming into contact with something higher, a higher level, a higher mind.

---

[9] Theophan the Recluse, Lorenzo Scupoli, Nicodemus of the Holy Mountain, *Unseen Warfare* (translated from the Russian by E. Kadloubovsky and G.E.H. Palmer). Faber and Faber Ltd., London, 1963.

It is ordained that man must put before all things the universal commandment — to remember God — of which it is said: "thou shalt remember the Lord thy God."[10] For, by the reverse of that which destroys us, we may be secure. What destroys us is forgetfulness of God, which shrouds the commandments in darkness and despoils us of all good.[11]

Yet, what is it that moves a man to prayer? We have suggested that, in the effort to relate to what is real, prayer must be something more, or let us better say, something "other" than an asking for whatever it is that the ordinary man in us does ask for - better living conditions, more money, finer friends, fame, power, and so forth.

And still, we see again and yet again that prayer, as we experience it, always breaks down, reduces to this very asking. Man prays because he wants something. I want. I pray. But who am "I"? And who will answer this "I"?

We are driven to ask: Can one truly pray with the ordinary mind, in an ordinary state? In order to pray, I must be different.

---

[10] New Testament, Deuteronomy 8:18.

[11] "Prayer of Jesus" from *Writings from the Philokalia on Prayer of the Heart* (translated from the Russian by E. Kadloubovsky and G.E.H. Palmer). Faber and Faber Ltd., London, 1954.

Man, knowing that he is lacking, that he is not, prays. And he begins to see that it is not his petition that is in question, his "I want" and "please give"; nor is it that to which he prays.

I, myself, am in question. Can it be that I pray to myself? To my real, my inner self? To that in me which is higher than my ordinary self, that which in fact is not ordinary, but extraordinary.

Our greatest need is to consecrate life through being faithful to a deeper reality in ourselves.[12] Can we see now that our prayer is for our birthright, lost and long forgotten, although not totally, for the memory of its taste is there, calling me, reminding me.

Man wishes not to pray as he would wish in his ordinary way; rather, he wishes for a state of prayer. He begins to realize the act of prayer.

We have suggested that prayer is a state, an active state, not a passive "asking." We see it as an active process, a process taking place in the one who prays.

This view is by no means unknown, though it is certainly not popular.

"Practice of the Jesus Prayer is the traditional

---

[12] Hugh L'Anson Pausset.

fulfillment of the injunction of the Apostle Paul to 'pray always'...."[13] It has been pointed out that "the Jesus Prayer...is...an intensely active process and is a scientific attempt to change the one who prays."[14]

But the question is how?

The spiritual exercise based on the Jesus Prayer, and known as Hesychasm, falls into three parts. First, "the prayer is repeated orally a specified number of times each day," in silence and solitude. Then it is "repeated silently in the mind an increased number of times during the day or night, and finally it is carried down into the heart using the rhythm of the heartbeats."[15]

From what we have said above I see that I must bring to prayer something in me that could correspond to that which I wish.

In order to begin to pray, I must first of all try to be contained. I must try not to be drawn by anything external, that is to say, by anything not corresponding to my aim, my prayer. Prayer, then, presupposes an inner order, a real wish.

I want. Yes. But it is now I who want. My

---

[13] *Philokalia*, Prayer of Jesus.
[14] *ibid*.
[15] *ibid*.

bigger I. No longer it wants, wishes, desires. I want.

And I pray. Now I can understand that the act of prayer is something beyond my ordinary self. I see that it is not my question that matters, but myself in the act of prayer that could give me the help for which I ask.

Prayer, like everything else in the universe, must be maintained. And it is I who maintain. Prayer without me, without my help, is no longer prayer.

On the way of self-perfection a man must not loiter for an instant. If he should stop for a moment working on himself he will slip back.[16]

My life is dead, but it could be alive in prayer. Is it not this that I seek? That state of prayer, of love, where I would be in touch with all that is.

With the idea of maintenance, I could begin in my very small way to understand something of the work of God. I could serve. For it is by maintenance that I can remain in a state of prayer. By this maintenance the laws of creation and the life of the universe exist.

---

[16] F. Ud-din Attar, *The Conference of the Birds* (translated by C.S. Nott). Janus Press, London, 1954.

"...nothing is wasted...."

WORK:
THE INNER DIMENSION

Mr. Gurdjieff once said, "When you exercise, do it as a service to the whole of humanity." What did he wish to convey?

When I ask myself, "How could I make my effort for the whole of humanity," I see that not only is the scale of my effort too small, but also that there is a greater dimension, a deeper implication, even in my personal efforts. That greater implication, apparently beyond my reach, needs somehow to be included, realized, in my work; otherwise it will not correspond to "school work."

What is this greater dimension? No words express it because it is not directly perceived through the senses; it is, however, perceived at moments by an inner awareness. Then questions arise: What is my "essence"? What is "imperishable being"?

The scale of my work is that of my actions, my inner responses to life at any moment. That response is mostly from my "personality," defined by Mr. Gurdjieff as that which has been acquired through life: "what is not my own." Because most action is based on what is not my own, it is weak, changeable, and I am aware of that. But in a crisis, in danger, I am strong; my whole being is engaged; there is strength and power in the essence when the call is sufficient to touch it. It is as though another dimension in myself was touched, the very depths of my being.

How to reach this depth? How to live and be guided by conscience and not by convenience? I need to live by that inner strength, and I see that all the time I am the slave of my automatic reactions.

It seems to be the result of the Law of Octaves that I cannot at will reach my depths. I begin to gather my attention, to concentrate, but I always come to the same point. Then something calls my attention, a thought, a memory, even just the awareness of my own more tranquil state; I find myself again in turning thoughts. So a training, a discipline, is necessary. It needs three aspects.

To take a simple example of this: I wish to go to Europe next year and decide to learn French; so I buy a dictionary and grammar and begin to study. But after a short time I find progress slow, my enthusiasm weakens, I tell myself there is not enough time for study and when there is I do not have the right energy available. So an "interval" comes and I lay aside my books. At that point, to continue effectively

I must find a class or at least one or two companions to give the study momentum. Again I am enthused, again get to a point where it is difficult to continue without hearing the language all around me. Finally, when I get to Europe this happens, and a real mastery of the language can appear.

This is an illustration of the discipline of school; it must have three aspects, three "inner dimensions" of different scales. One is work by myself; a second is work with others, the group; the third, work for the school, "for humanity." These three aspects together ensure that the intervals (due to the Law of Octaves) in each aspect are overcome, and the work continues effectively to reach its aim.

But is it as easy as that? Not in practice, because the three are all simultaneous; these three inner dimensions are connected and must act on each other for the result to be attained. So one cannot work on just one, then another, then the last. Mr. Gurdjieff also expressed it: "work must be for yourself, for the group and for me" (that is, for the school). It can begin in any place, but must soon develop to touch all three aspects.

Each line involves suffering: suffering at seeing what I am, my nothingness; suffering at working with others, seeing that we do not understand one another except superficially, that we do not love one another, that we even think or say malicious things behind the back of another; suffering for our complacency and passivity; finally, suffering for the human condition, for those who are swallowed up in misery, poverty, crime, ignorance.

It is this suffering which brings about a connection with another dimension, with inner depths; it is that elusive quality, sincerity with myself, which brings about contact with "being," the truth in myself. And so the suffering of each aspect of school work brings not only suffering but also a subtle joy — because to know the truth, to understand, always brings positive feeling: "In the space around thought, love is born."

Because these three hidden dimensions exist, an esoteric school is pictured by Mr. Gurdjieff as a monastery he had visited in Asia with three courtyards: in the outermost are those belonging to exoteric groups; in the middle court, mesoteric; in the inner courtyard, those of the esoteric circle. The gate of the outer court connects with ordinary life; it is a place of novitiate testing. The middle court is in direct contact with both the outer and inner circles, with those being tested and those who know, those who have already passed through discipline.

Life there is hard; those in the middle court are "between two stools," awake to many defects in themselves but not yet in harmony with themselves; not yet able to live from essence. In the innermost court there is depth: both being and understanding, harmony and knowledge, action directed toward an aim.

LETTERS

to

his pupils

London
27 Sept. 1971

Dear Mr. T.K.,

I think what you say about your attempts at meditation shows that it is difficult to learn about consciousness from books. The fact that after trying it you gave it up, because it seemed too passive a way, shows that. Also that you have taken to using smoking marijuana shows the same. It is the very worst thing for you to do, from the viewpoint of increasing your consciousness.

You certainly cannot give up your studies for the "Work," because the work of "self-study" and "self-knowledge" cannot be done outside your own normal life, where you are most "yourself."

For the moment, you can read or re-read, for example, *The Psychology of Man's Possible Evolution* by P. D. Ouspensky, as a help for self-study. Try to come (as you suggest) and see me when I am next in Chicago.

With very kind regards.
Sincerely,

Christopher Fremantle

New York
22 January 1972

Dear T.,

There is a serious misunderstanding which must be cleared up. It is pure imagination to think that you are "self-conscious" all day; for the present you must give up all thought of work towards consciousness during your whole day except for 20 minutes in the morning which you devote to sitting in good, upright posture, deep relaxation, trying to find your own inner silence.

Apart from that one effort, which must be most strictly limited to the time, lead the most normal student life you can. Study and forget about everything else for now — write me again —

Sincerely yours,

C. Fremantle

Jan. 26

Dear T.,

Thank you for taking the pains to write your impressions. The "idiot" in the dervish movement is perhaps one of the most difficult things of all to do. The attention of the class and their precision and the way they were able to move together came from their state of attention.

Mrs. F. did not mean the movements were changing, of course, but that the work on them of the classes is always changing — when one thing has been learned, one aspect of their work, then the class can approach another aspect; this is hard to realize, at times, when it is myself working in a class.

Sincerely yours,

Christopher Fremantle

41 East 59th St.
New York, NY 10022
March 8 (1973)

Dear S.,

Perhaps by the time you get this you will know what "fate" has decided in terms of your firm's contract. What matters is one's orientation. We cannot control individual moods perhaps, but if one's choice corresponds to a constant orientation, the very movement of life helps one to go towards one's aim.

It is strange that the meeting with your father which has been accomplished, now that you have to leave soon, has severed itself, apparently. Perhaps it may be better that way; something has been done, and evidently for the moment that is all that has proved possible. Later, perhaps, there will be a new possibility.

You speak about the difficulty of sustaining your work. What is most difficult for a long time is to be sure of the value of your inner attention. We gather this at moments, and then it is not able to resist the attraction of the movement of life and quickly evaporates. For this reason, we do not become aware of its power as a force which will bring the centers into connection and make possible a harmonious and stable relation between them. I need the testimony of others working in the same way to be sure this is not simply a subjective view.

It is this force which creates new steps in the metabolism, and lends it the material possibility of new states of consciousness. Of course you are right about the connection between fears, the psyche and some health questions; but this is therapy, and the Work goes far beyond that into the question of becoming conscious, which is touching another level. Health requires the right functioning on the level we are on; the Work is touching levels beyond this, and the chief means — as we can prove very well to ourselves — is the struggle for a centered inner attention. It is this which creates a new substance, that links our usual faculties with finer levels of thought and feeling.

        Affectionate thoughts.
        Yours,

        C.F.

41 East 59th St.
New York, NY 10022
Dec. 10th, '72

Dear J.,

The need to understand our emotional life is because the force for a new state, which could survive the pressures of life, is in the emotions — the head is not capable of that alone. This understanding cannot be reached by work in the form of meetings alone quickly enough, and we need many experiences together for that.

With very warm regards and thoughts as always to you both,

Christopher Fremantle

41 East 59th Street
New York 10022

Dear J.,

It is a help when someone tells honestly about their reaction to a new form, or to an effort, and without that it is hard to know.

In any case I saw the movements class — it was not easy for anyone and quite hard for many. To know that it brought life to the subsequent meeting was very good. I hope it may be the beginning of a helpful work between the "South Side" and "Chicago" groups in the future.

We too saw the Dervishes here. I had seen them in Paris twice and had even learned, long ago, to do the turning. Whether watching, or participating in whatever way, one sees the force of an inner effort to affect others and bring a new vibration in the world.

We need these testimonies to give us the courage to work on, even if the results seem sometimes far away.

With best wishes and
warm regards to you both,

Christopher Fremantle

Saturday May 1st
7:30 a.m.

Dear J.,

"To work in the best possible way"...the Way is the safe road for all, an interior way leading from our automatic state to a conscious inner life. There is no outer way and really there can be none.

But because I am not able in my (low) present state to live only by the inner light, I try to surround myself with other situations which remind me, provoke me, challenge me to live by that inner light and find it again when lost. This is the Way's outer aspect.

Sincerely,

Christopher Fremantle

American Airlines
Mexico, D.F. 20
Monday
June 18, 1973

Dear J.,

    L. feels much concerned for the state of the group and is fearful that some of its members may leave very soon.

    It was a small meeting since you and your wife and also N. were absent. But I must say that I had a good impression and felt that all those present feel the need for something like that in their lives.

    I'm not sure, but it seems to me that she felt there is sometimes not enough initiative from B. While I respect and have great confidence in him, it is possible she is right. He cannot do everything alone. She feels that if she were to bring more initiative it would not be so well received, as if, for example, it came from you. She is possibly right about that, too.

    It took me a long time to realize for myself that in spite of a wholly sincere feeling of inadequacy, which I share, among people generally when they take part in the Work, its progress still depends on everyone in the group.

I feel the South Side group is important to the growth of work of this kind in Chicago, both now, and also for the sake of the Friday reading group B. has started, which contains some very fine people including your son. They will need to be helped by the older group when the time comes.

For these reasons I am writing to you quite privately to ask if you can help L., and myself, too, to bring what is necessary. I am sure the other members of the group will all be grateful to you if the Work is maintained well till more understanding appears.

With very warm regards
and good wishes,

Christopher Fremantle

July 23, 1973

Dear J.,

...What you say will help you to understand better the role of a group.

You have seen, with the eyes of conscience, the situation. That awakening of conscience is what the Work exists for; you owe it in part, as you confess, to the group, even if the group is lethargic, and seem to be in their "bomb shelters." Finally each one is free and you are not responsible for them; your responsibility is for yourself. So do not be concerned about their state, except that you need them to help you, and they, perhaps, need you and your understanding. If they do not, that too is their business.

I, too, think that readings from Nicoll are not a good basis for work at this point: the only way to learn is by a task which is undertaken voluntarily and of which, as Gurdjieff said, "that is your God," "you give yourself your word" — while you are undertaking it. I thought you could help in finding more nourishing ways to work, and in helping to bring a basis of *observations*, and not "discussion," which is too easy. It is the exchange of experiences, not of commentaries, which brings life. Try always, as you do, to work during the meetings — not to meditate, but to be as entirely present as possible to yourself and to everything that takes place and to the life of exchange you bring.

You can count on L., and there is another woman in the Friday reading group, who also you will meet in due course, who feels as you do. With two or three people everything will come to life.

Do not try to supplant B. He has formed the group; try to be a complement to him — he cannot alone — as you also cannot alone — bring all that is necessary.

Please write to me when you wish and I will be very glad.

Always yours sincerely,

Christopher Fremantle

If you can bring what you need, the "others" will be grateful to you one day in a way you do not expect, or merit, probably.

Mexico
August 22, '73

Dear J.,

I was so glad to hear that there had been some new vibrations in the meeting of the group. Nothing remains the same for long, and this constant effort of renewal has to be brought intentionally again and again. It is a great help to me to feel there are two or three people who feel the need for that, who make that attempt.

Here we are having an active time, but the same conflict between inertia and conscience manifests itself continually, and there is the need not to be influenced by these rises and falls, but to keep one's regard on the goal, without being unduly distracted by one's own inevitable reactions.

With warmest regards,

Christopher Fremantle

41 East 59th St.
N.Y.C. 10022
23 October '73

Dear J.,

...The circulation of people and of ideas is helpful. What we are is the most important study — what I am is shown not by what I think, but by what I do. Self-observation in the trivia of daily life is the best way to know what I am: it is always a humbling experience, and is the only thing which leads to the bedrock from which growth can occur. That is what Nicoll's *Commentaries* are all about.

But because reading can make one neglect the real work of observation, I never personally recommend anyone to read Nicoll's *Commentaries* as a basis for work, though I admire and respect their sincerity. So if observation is gradually replacing reading, that is a good direction.

Incidentally, Nicoll must have thought in the same way, or he would himself have published them. He did not; but his pupils after his death decided to do that, and we have to be grateful to them just the same.

Sincerely,

Christopher Fremantle

41 East 59
New York 10022
Oct. 25th, 1974

Dear J.,

I have the impression that this year has been probably the most difficult in your experience, and I take everything you write in view of that supposition, which may, however, be wrong.

You write about *metanoia*, the need for a change of mind, and it is one of the things needed, but man cannot change one thing unless other things change too (except for a short time by a great effort, and this is not the change needed); so a change of mind will mean also a change of body, and above all, a change of feeling, so that even a small change is a big accomplishment.

You feel your own helplessness, but you do not admit the others, perhaps, are equally helpless. You feel their complacency, try to show it to them, and demand that they see it and agree. When this fails, you feel intolerant, but you tolerate your own weaknesses because you cannot do otherwise until they have been changed.

At present we need to see, and the group can be like mirrors for us. We need their help to see our own weakness, not their help by being righteous or wrathful; nor do they need ours in that way.

And now you write of being severe with yourself, as you are with them. I do not know what you intend by this, but it may prove better at times to laugh at yourself than to be severe!

What do I call "myself"? So many things, but which is the Self?

I need to be infused, illumined by a Truth.

It is good really to stay away for a time, a few months perhaps. During this time I will be glad, as always, to talk together when I stay overnight in Chicago. Gradually things will change perhaps and you will see your way more clearly.

Enclosed is a manuscript I had access to from a friend in Argentina a few years ago. I think you will like it.

> With all good wishes and
> warm regards,
>
> Christopher Fremantle

41 East 59th Street
1/17/75

Dear J.,

You write about seeing your "inner criticism" and when it will be "abated." Please think more, if you can, about what it is to *be free*. The moment of critical judgment is bound to be there — but what happens the next moment? Can I be free from it? I know it, but it does not attach itself to me.

Yes — people are not as they should be; above all, I am not as I should be...but when I see it, know it, and realize it *is so*, the call is for *action*, not for further criticism. Here all my attention, my collected state, are required to act with wisdom and discretion; I am dealing with facts, not pursuing opinions mentally.

All my wishes,

Christopher

Sunday

Dear J.,

Thank you for your letter. Afterwards before going to sleep I was reading the chapter "Peter Karpenko" in *Meetings with Remarkable Men*. Better than rereading my old letters, which contain so little wisdom, read that chapter, which is so full of it.

With very affectionate regards,

Christopher Fremantle

Excerpt from a letter:

Obedience covers all principles, but is mainly connected with one main idea, that of verification. This system teaches that you must verify everything you see, hear and feel and only in that way can you come to something. According to Gurdjieff, the sooner a man begins to verify all that he hears, the better for him. The important thing about rules is to realize that there is only one rule, one principle: one must not do anything unnecessary. Until you have understood this, you have to try rules which are given. But to do something only because you are told — is a form of laziness. People believe or disbelieve when they are too lazy to think. In the Work people use the same methods they use in life. They adapt — try to make work as comfortable as possible, or at least as little uncomfortable as possible — and in that way they lose what the Work can give. Adapting in life may be right in certain areas — but adapting in the Work is always wrong. Time is counted. If people do not work seriously enough, it is a waste of time.

C.F.

41 East 59th St.
N.Y.C. 10022
7/7/76

Dear J.,

The big effort by the group and by J. and the others from here has evoked something of the real "current of work" which we need so much to participate in, and to sustain us at times.

It is always there, somewhere in our depths, but it needs to permeate gradually all our functions, even our "ego," and give it a different resonance, to become another law influencing our lives. It is only at times of relatively intensive work, that one is permeated by it and realizes, by experience, that this law is not artificial, but the most natural thing — only, it is on another (interior) level.

Next weekend we have such a "three days" of work here, and I hope to share in that experience, having been excluded by circumstance from sharing it with you all. We need to be enlivened by that shared current from time to time and to be refreshed by it, until it is able to create an inner order which will be stronger than the accidental impacts of life.

With affectionate regards,
J., as always,

Christopher Fremantle

Mexico
September 5, 1972

Dear A.F.,

...You ask about a man receiving direct help on different levels. It is important to realize that the help man needs is provided by nature who also planned for his growth within himself. What seems to be, and is, help from outside is effective because it awakes resonances within him. This can take place on different levels.

With kind regards as always,

Christopher Fremantle

41 East 59th St.
N.Y.C. 10022
2/21/73

Dear F.,

...One realizes that one is capable of a much more full state of consciousness, that there is no organic reason to be so asleep.

There are many kinds of shocks. When life gives a strong shock, as in this case, you are aware of it. But many shocks which come from life are wasted through lack of preparation. For example, someone gets angry with me: all that results is self-justification. Why cannot that shock serve to waken me? Because I have no prepared attitude in my mind to such a shock, no wish that I would receive it to awaken myself.

The *group* also exists to give shocks.

I doubt if you can create them today — you must try, however, to make use of what nature sends you every day. Later on we will learn to create shocks, perhaps.

About the thought of death, it is a good direction to work in — you cannot expect to change a lifetime habit of ignoring it in a few days.

With sincere regards,

Christopher Fremantle

3/7/73

Dear F.,

It is important to keep in focus the outside while studying the inside. Do not let self-remembering become introversion.

Self-criticism is in reference to my actions in outer situations for the most part. It is destructive when it is negative and inflates me when it is positive. Both forms are a kind of egoism.

You can only become relatively free from it by seeing it clearly in reference to the outside to which it refers and by trying to stay with the spontaneous impulse (of remorse) from which it starts — which is quite different and positive.

Sincerely yours,

Christopher Fremantle

4/5/73

Dear F.,

    Depressions have many sources and only you can say the causes of yours, which can be "psychological" or "physio-chemical." As you saw, the only immediate way is not to believe in them as the whole of you, not to identify with them. Study them and what makes them appear.

    In the same way, when you see you always act "big," try not to be negative but to study it. Why? I do not feel my own presence; but the need to feel an "I" is there, and not knowing how to search for the real "I" feeling, I content myself with a substitute, which gives me a sense of security.

                            Sincerely,

                              C.F.

5/16/73

Dear F.,

You are right in thinking that the Work is a way of life, just as music is.

At every moment some work is possible. There is something that can be seen and some new understanding which can come.

However, skills which are necessary for earning a living are delicately balanced combinations of the centers. Playing an instrument, for example. These more or less mechanical adaptations are fragile: a bad cold will upset them because the instinctive center is upset. So also, if you try with your head to remember yourself, then, your playing will not be so fine.

If you work at your living for 8 hours and sleep for 8 hours, there are still 8 for work on yourself. That is enough if you really are able to make use of them...patience!

Warm regards to you as always,

C.F.

41 East 59th St.
New York City 10022
7 February '74

Dear F.,

Don't think I said "become empty" within — impossible because "nature abhors a vacuum" — but make space, space for a new way of living and experiencing, to grow, perhaps.

You are quite right — the inner authority — the voice of conscience — the need is there. The "guru" has always said he is there temporarily, until the inner authority is able to be heard and to become the source of action.

With affectionate thoughts,

Christopher Fremantle

4/20/74

Dear F.,

    To understand the facts of the centers it is necessary to observe how the degree of attention given in an action affects the workings of a particular center.

    Try to move into much attention, doing some physical work; or try to think with much attention — but with awareness — not "thought-attention."

    You will see that when you pay attention closely for a certain time the action changes in quality. When you have some observations that are clear bring them to the group.

                              Kind regards,

                                      C.F.

Mexico
July 11, '74

Dear F.,

...You could read in *Views from the Real World* notes of a lecture beginning "How Can We Gain Attention?" Mr. Gurdjieff is so simple and so direct.

It is a good realization if you see that every situation can be looked at, from one aspect, as a question of attention.

I hope that everything is well with the group. I suppose you will be moving at a slow rhythm with no visits from W., etc., for a time.

Many good thoughts,

Christopher Fremantle

Mexico
1 August

Dear F.,

Certainly *Beelzebub* is different when read aloud; it only discloses its wisdom drop by drop as response to one's wish to understand.

About "buffers," the real way to pull them down is through tasks undertaken in the name of one's work. You will see gradually it is the best way. This is why we need a common practical work, with responsibilities, such as a house might help to bring.

I am very glad you will be having a work day together on August 4th, and I hope that it will help to bring a feeling of need for such experiences more regularly.

With very kind regards to you and your wife,

Christopher Fremantle

Mexico
Aug. 16th

Dear F.,

Ouspensky at one time gave all our groups an exercise to sit for 5 minutes and try to stop our thoughts, and then for 5 minutes to try to think about some idea of the Work — e.g., "man cannot do," "the law of 3," "knowledge and being," and so on. I do not have the whole program here — so cannot send it. I found the practice showed me my inability to think and helped me very much.

Yes! What was it Gurdjieff called "active mentation"? Only experience will answer this question!

Do not attach too much importance to the so-called "lotus position." The Hindus have a body adapted to that; the Chinese and Japanese always had a problem in imitating this "squatting," as the Chinese called it. In the West it is not our natural posture since we use chairs. However, it has many merits for this work. The important things are to be able to have the back straight, the breathing quite unhampered, the head poised, the body relaxed. Sometimes it is useful to work against pain, but not if it renders everything else impossible.

I'm glad the time of no meeting is a time when you can devote yourself to a personal work.

Here we are just beginning a period of intensive work on movements, and it will be for about three weeks. I hope it will prove interesting.

With very kind regards.
Sincerely,

Christopher Fremantle

2/4/75

Dear F.,

    I do not know what you call a "significant" inner experience. Every experience we have is an inner experience, and everything has its significance. Even if, as you say, you had no experience in one year which "has significance," that too is significant.

    Sometimes, accidentally, some factors are aligned and there is a new and "significant" experience, which may show the direction one is working in is right.

    The difficulty created is just the one you are writing about — I begin to feel I should have these, I have a right to them, and if not, something is wrong. This is a change of position, indeed, from the feeling of gratitude, of not having merited it, which special experiences usually bring.

    In the final event, "what we sow we reap." The farmer puts in his winter wheat and does not expect results beyond a small green shoot till spring. We too are dealing with big events, on a longer time scale.

                              With affectionate regards.
                              Sincerely,

                              Christopher Fremantle

9/21/75

Dear F.,

    I agree with the direction of your experiments to try to "think" in a better way. Ideas from another level are a help to this. But do not try too hard. Try, and try often, but do not think you can force anything. You cannot.

    When you begin to find a quiet lucid state from which to begin, and you find a real wish (not reaction and frustration), you will find something appear just a little at a time.

                             Yours,

                             Christopher Fremantle

3/17/76

Dear F.,

You will see that to be free from expressing negativeness is not to be free from it. On the contrary, often you simply suppress the negativeness, and its energy is not at all helpful then.

So work on the attitude of mind, and at the same time try to see why the reaction is negative, when it is useless and harmful and I know it. Sometimes try not to express, at other times try to let it go its way and watch it, without losing yourself, if you are able.

About "sitting" in the evening, all the alternatives you mention are good, but only if you do one of them, not several at once.

The problem is to know what and who I am, not only in action, but also in my very depths apart from action, apart from outside life. Always be active when you "sit" even if it is just with the physical sensation; never passive.

This too we can speak about, better than write.

With kind regards.
Sincerely,

Christopher Fremantle

New York
7/14/76

Dear F.,

I was interested by what you wrote, that is, the discovery that to pass on your experience to others is a way of coming to a new understanding of it for oneself. That is a very precious thing, but it can only be experienced, or shared, with another who has also experienced it; otherwise to speak about it has no sense.

But you see that in a good group each gains from the *exchange of experience* — there are no "answers"— only questions raised by experience and understanding arising from the attempt to look sincerely at the experience and its significance, whatever it is.

This calls one to see that the relation in a group is quite specifically for that, and diluting it with personal relationships in other spheres (e.g., business, hobbies, sex, etc.) lowers its level to the ordinary, and is finally unnecessary. You have to discourage it in yourself and also among those working together (allowing for the fact that some may have a prior relationship, which is how they came to the group, and so are part of this work situation).

Well, "karma" is a narrow idea. The truth is we are in a current of vast forces which come from the past and carry us impotently wherever they carry us. To ascribe all that to my past lives is just another lie and expression of my egoism, though that too *may be* a factor — but the mechanical movement dominates that. Mr. Gurdjieff expressed his view in "the two rivers" in the last part of *Beelzebub*, and in a talk in *Views*.

Yes — perhaps your wife is making an angel out of you, but I hope too you are making one of her, and by the same means!

Sincerely,

Christopher Fremantle

6/17/77

Dear F.,

I received your letter detailing your many experiences working on a composition commissioned for TV.

They show the extraordinary range between the mechanical and the more conscious aspects of thinking and feeling.

Is it possible to simply regard this experience as material, without drawing any conclusions now? Begin to try to investigate experimentally, in attempting other compositions, the reasons and nature of the changes — other than being simply the "swing of the pendulum." This is the only possible way of reaching an "objective" view. Certainly what you describe has nothing to do with the "second conscious shock" since it all simply happened.

>With warm regards to you both.
>Sincerely,
>
>Christopher Fremantle

11/29/77

Dear F.,

When you give yourself your word (in your work's name), *nothing* should make you break it. If it is broken, some integrity in you is broken. The early Christians were thrown to the lions in the arena rather than break their word. Can you be like that?

You give yourself your word not to smoke — say — between 8 and 9 a.m. and you *do not break it*. After you can do that, and your body is accustomed to it, you should extend it to 9:30. Tell me what you do and I will try to help you.

Even from the basest motives, you should do this, if you do not wish to have a lung removed in a few years' time.

Good wishes,

Christopher Fremantle

2/19/78

Dear F.,

    Yes! One's idea of "work" must be always changing as one gains experience, and I am sure the experience brought by your grandmother's death can have been a help towards that kind of change. It does not mean that "work" as understood before was wrong, but that one has found something more true than before was possible.

    To be more aware often brings the feeling of "not knowing." "Knowing" in the usual sense is our security; we cling to it for dealing with life and its call. Beginning to awake, one is deeply aware one "knows" only the surface of oneself — the real nature must be rediscovered.

    With all good wishes,

    Christopher Fremantle

June 21st

Dear F.,

You are quite right — it is possible to collect and retain for a while in activity, some fine energy brought by active attention to physical sensation.

The Jesus prayer is an advanced technique, and needs to be taught by an experienced teacher, as your negative experience shows clearly.

I would think that an effort to "ponder" is much more useful than "repetition" of a mantra — this also is not done in the right way (actively) — but the fact you felt a "lightness" after trying to ponder shows that some new and fine energy was gained through this, and it opens an important direction.

How to be "active"? And from where?

This is something we need to come to and I will try to open this question more when I come.

With very kind regards.
Sincerely,

Christopher Fremantle

41 East 59th Street
New York, N.Y. 10022
May 29th

Dear H.,

Thank you for writing to me, which I so much appreciated, to tell me how you have been touched by Madame de Salzmann's preface to *Views from the Real World*. I wish she would write about Mr. Gurdjieff out of her vast store of memories and deep understanding, and she has said she will, but when will she have time to do that?

I hope the summer will not be a complete stop of group work together. I do not like these vacations — our time is too short — but when many people go away, as they do in New York, there is nothing else possible. I look forward to seeing you on the 14th.

With kind regards
and best to you both.
As always,

Christopher

Mexico
June 24th '75

Dear N.,

It is interesting to work in a group the way you have been trying in Group 3.[17] I did this in various groups, at Madame de Salzmann's suggestion, for at least 4 years, before trying to "lead" any group, and I was most grateful for having been given the experience.

It is not really a matter of having "answers" — since they are less important than the "questions" in some respects. Properly speaking, a group is for exchange of observations; what is necessary for the "older one" to do is bring his or her *own experiences* in regard to the matter being spoken about. Without doing first what you are attempting, one may have years of "work" experiences, but not have ready access to them in one's memory or thoughts. To try to find one's own valid experiences in one's mind, untroubled by the need to speak at first, is a good preparation. I am glad you appreciate working with B. and C., and the differences of their approaches. Each person must find his own way to relate to a group — to that particular group, and those particular people. Also, if one of them cannot sometime attend, you might be a precious support for the one who remains there, if you know the group and the individuals well.

---

[17] That is, sitting in front as an assistant to the leader and not speaking.

The most important thing in a group is to be able to be present to oneself and to the group. Without that, all the rest has only relative value.

Now that there is a "vacation," i.e., change of pace, you can try to make the moment of work in silence, alone, at the beginning of each day, the time for gathering of contact with one's own deep inner tranquility, so that the day's activities can be related, directly or indirectly, to that state of *active* calm. The sensing of the body will be a helpful link.

The group here is a great support to me and I am very content to be with them again, and to continue work instead of having a so-called vacation.

With kind regards.
Sincerely,

Christopher Fremantle

Tijuana, Mexico
12/1/76

Dear R.,

Yes, it is horrifying to see how little attention I have. All my idea of myself comes from the moments of attention I remember — the inattention leaves no impression. So my idea of myself is wholly unreal. Only seeing deeply what you describe will change this automatic attitude toward myself into a real wish to know myself.

What I got from the talks with Madame in N.Y. was the importance of "seeing" — it is that which brings change — yet the moment I see something new it distracts me and so I do not go on seeing long enough for a deep impression to be received. So how to go on...

With all affectionate
wishes to you and G.
and many thoughts,

Christopher Fremantle

N.Y.C.
11/28/77

Dear R.,

What you write about "connection with what I know" touches familiar ground. For example, from 1941 to 1956 I could read Spanish fluently and "knew" a vast vocabulary. When in 1956 I had to speak it (which I had never done), not a word was "connected"; I couldn't find any of them.

It is the same with a group. I was in 1950 protesting at having to lead a group, and Mrs. H. said to me, "but you must have a great deal of material." It was the same thing — I had, but I could not "connect" with it. But faced with a group, it gradually came into focus. It is one of the great blessings which comes from facing a group of "younger" people — that it brings back and clarifies one's own vague and dormant experience and makes it accessible to one's growing understanding.

What you send about color and the enneagram also evokes many experiences. For a few months when I was in Paris I tried to find a way to use the combinations arriving through the enneagram, but really without any tangible satisfaction.

One thing is that the whole range of visible light is only one octave — and the enneagram is based on the interaction of three octaves, as it occurs in life phenomena.

Also the harmonies which occur in music are based on more than one octave — apart from the basic *do mi la do* and so on. I never found shades of color corresponding to musical harmony, though if one knew the Angstrom wavelengths one might be able. Also even pure paints are not pure colors. So harmonies are more easily approached by emotional sensibility than by mathematical analysis.

It is quite evident that the triangle

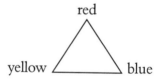

represents symbolically or emotionally the triangle

but granted that, where does one go to from there?

What always interested me, in color, was Mr. Gurdjieff's note that emotional effects were in variation within one tone — I find it true both in his own playing of his "harmonium" (hand organ) and in color — in weaving, for example.

With affectionate thoughts
to you both always,

C.F.

N.Y.C.
1/28

Dear R.,

So glad you are coming up for even a short visit, and can maintain touch with the groups here.

The time Madame is going to be here, I understand, is through February and part of March.

It would be difficult to summarize here what she has given in the groups — more an understanding of a point of view perhaps than a very specific task.

L. told me she had heard from you and was hoping you may be with them, which will be a great asset for a short visit.

I know from my summers in Mexico, how working only with a younger group makes one realize the need for a continuing exchange with one's own companions. I am glad the group is growing because the challenge grows too with it....

Affectionate thoughts to you both and the E.'s as always,

Christopher Fremantle

N.Y.C.
May 15th

Dear R.,

I see from your letter that you are completely self-centered about the Work; you do not say anything about your group leader's difficulties with her age, health, understanding, difficulties with yourselves and this group which Providence has sent her from nowhere; nothing but your subjective feelings of discomfort with her and comfort with the E.'s. Since when did you expect the Work to be a bed of roses? And finding thorns, you now propose to hand them to me and look for roses elsewhere? A new young group? Perhaps rosebuds; the thorns will surely appear again later....

One difficulty is that you forget that you and your group leader are trying to follow the same ascending current. In that current, you cannot be in conflict. You reduce this relationship to the personal level: like and dislike. You cannot expect to like her when you come close, or to be liked by her. She does not expect to like you either and never did, perhaps. But she will work with you and you can work with her; it is an inner thing; nothing can stop it. It is the only thing that is possible; in it there is no conflict, but there is mutual support. You can work with G. and B. when your personality is put aside and you can with her when you do that. Another thing you are not aware of is that she evidently understands work with people of different stages of development better than you do.

When people first come to the work, they are not able to see themselves at all. Everything is confused between what they see and what they imagine and expect to see. They cannot get a fresh start. They have no relationship with sensation, such as you and your husband have through dance. At the Prieure Mr. G. gave very hard physical work, from 6AM to evening, even to middle-aged intellectuals, and if you study you will see many traditions do the same. Why? Not because he needed cows, pigs and vegetables, but because it was very important to establish a relation between his pupils and their own bodies before anything else was possible. "Everything is body," he said. In the evening, there were talks and movements and eating, but only after exhausting daily work. Month after month.

It is important to remember this if you organize work for "new" people — up to 2 or 3 years at least. The things you did, which might be right for you, are absolutely wrong and even harmful for the new people. They need to get tired, struggle against their body reactions, laziness, self-pity; begin to breathe normally and eat normally; through "work days" to learn what it is to have a body. Making kites, drama, form and color, etc., is a pure waste of time for them and so for you. Your group leader sensed this and stopped it all as quickly as possible. (Later — that will be another phase.) You completely misunderstood her motives and should even thank the man with a gun for reporting. You see, it comes from inexperience combined with egoism. You do not see what they need, and you think they can receive from the same things as you — they cannot, today, and it will turn against you and they will leave disappointed.

What I suggest is that when your group leader returns, you tell her it was a mistake for you to organize the work days, but that they are needed. Ask her to give you exact instructions what is to be done, and try to do it exactly, impersonally, as an exercise to understand her point of view and your own narrow subjectivity. If she says L. will be in charge, then L. will be in charge, 100%, and you do exactly what she indicates. You will then have a real work on yourself. Do not try to work together 4 times a day; do this instead, it will be more balanced. Work once a day if you can manage. Remember it is all inner work and no outside conditions can make it impossible.

...It is useless to give up working with the group and will leave you in the void — go right on and profit by your mistakes. If you are watchful you will learn not only what to do, but what not to do. Never accept anything blindly even if it is from somebody far ahead, and question everything. Relate to your group leader, then you will see it is not a question of agreeing or disagreeing — that is all just our thoughts and feelings. Relation is from Being.

Dear R., I will write your husband a note too. I am so glad you wrote though correspondence is a laborious way to communicate.

> Affectionate thoughts
> and love to you both,
>
> Christopher Fremantle

P.S. About meetings and the new group, at first words are important — if your group leader is wordy, it may be right for them; later one's relation with words changes. She stays very close to Ouspensky's way at the start, I feel, and it is quite sound (if you cannot be a Madame de S.).

N.Y.C.
10/31

Dear R.,

It must be interesting to work again with your group leader and to come back to it on a new level where even the difficulties are positive in their action on work. I sympathize with your decision to stay outside of any gossip in the group. The sound rule in a group (which we were given by Ouspensky) is that nobody may speak about another either behind his back (ever) or in front of him (except if specifically invited to). This is to be "as though" we are able to have conscience, perhaps. In any case I see the destructive effects of careless and thoughtless gossip in a group which exists for quite another purpose. If allowed, people use a group for everything — personal, social, business — without discrimination. It is always destructive of the real aim and purpose. Ouspensky understood that rules are given to show us that we are incapable of keeping them.

With many affectionate
thoughts and regards to
your husband, and
yourself, always,

Christopher Fremantle

June 2

Dear B.,

...I received the notes of the meeting you wrote about. It is important to remember, and is everywhere forgotten, that people come to the group with their own question, and when too much time is spent in a dialogue on one question the others who are present tend to get bored & even to feel they wasted their time in coming. For this reason, although I appreciate the freedom you speak about, it also must be accompanied by a consideration for the whole group, and a discrete constraint. In general we speak too much in the groups and say too little.

You cannot change things in relationships directly by being courageous and just telling how "you" feel; the "person" who does that is always a little part of oneself, and not the whole. When there is a real presence, this in itself is the biggest factor in changing the relationships in the way you so rightly wish to see them change, much more than what is said. Never let things degenerate into argument....

With very warm thoughts and good wishes to you both.

Affectionately,

C.F.

N.Y.C.
April 12

Dear B.,

...Your letter made me very happy that you have seen how you cannot "tell" people anything unless they ask; it is true, and it explains the difficulty of the transmission of work, and the miracle which Mr. Gurdjieff did in this respect.

In fact it is not words which "tell" — it is the emanation of being which is in constant speech. As Ramana Maharishi[18] once said, "speaking is continual silence, and silence is continual speech."

It is good there is a feeling of deep dissatisfaction in the group, provided it is positive and does not degenerate into negativeness, self-pity and despair. It is there that you can help — the voice of silence inside one does not admit either fear or doubt. Perhaps you can help C. to be aware of this, and that his sense of dissatisfaction is based on a truth, but this truth is positive....

C.F.

---

[18] Arthur Osborne (Ed.), *Collected Works of Ramana Maharishi*. Rider and Co., London, 1959.

N.Y.C.
26 April

Dear B.,

...I am glad you find yourself able to work better in the calm. That is what has gradually to infuse our active life, to give it direction and sense.

Christopher

N.Y.C.
5/16

Dear B.,

The work proposed by your group leader seems very helpful to you as well as to the group. One discovers that one does not really understand these laws, it is all with the formatory part; and the centers, one needs to know their working by taste, the different energies, the different qualities. Work for yourself in the framework of the group...call on them to help your study, without saying so openly, and then the exchange will help them too. Consider them in seeing they need the presence of a real work.

Don't tell yourself "it's easy to see why the work has never gotten hold here." It is very slow, difficult and arduous to give it a hold, everywhere. But it is the way to verify and prove the understanding....

                              With very affectionate
                              thoughts and greetings
                              to you both as always,

                              C.F.

N.Y.C.
10/3

Dear B.,

It seems more and more clear to me the principle of 3 runs through the maintenance of all life, including the life of the work. A plant dies if one of its 3 foods is absent. It's the same with work, the "3 lines" are three sources of life. Even a "bad" relation with the group gives food, perhaps more than a "good" one!

Love to you both,

C.F.

N.Y.C.
Oct. 25th

Dear B.,

It is splendid you felt for a moment a real acceptance of you and R. in the group, but don't please have the illusion it will be permanent. Try to remember a "bad" relationship is often as useful for my work as a "good" one, or even better, because it shows many undesirable features in sharp relief. When there is awakening it is continuously revealing "bad" and "good," and that is consciousness....

...Projects are useful as a means of being together. I am glad something is going on and I hope it has a sense for you. You see this is not realized by all the group; nothing in the work comes very quickly....

C.F.

New York
12 Dec. 1971

Dear B.,

Your letter speaks about the random movements in myself which obscure the real, spontaneous movement that is only seen when I am collected, and that needs to ascend within myself.

The projects are what they are. The kind of experience you speak about makes one feel a real humility for what I am, and that is important. One needs to be brought to it again and again. The days of work, crafts, etc., can do that. The outward results are less important than these inner impressions, the truth about the human condition. When I feel my nullity, I am related to the eternal; my feeling of "myself," in the sense of ego, cuts me off from that.

You need your wish to be liked to help you in relating to the group, so don't despise it; their "friendliness" continually reminds you how not to be. But outwardly you need "friendliness," since that is the language they understand.

Yes, I am glad the day of work was crowded. People do not realize what work means — they want to come so close and no closer to each other. Mr. G. had 70 people in his small apartment in the Wellington, cooked for them, talked with them. What suffering! But it was quite voluntary — he could have escaped it. It seems to me that he was teaching us by example, though at the time I took it all for granted.

    Please do not reject being in Chicago; Mr. Gurdjieff's work is important anywhere it exists, and we are very closely linked by that; the distance is all illusion....

C.F.

N.Y.C.
May 15, 1976

Dear B.,

I put a reply to your earlier letter in the mail. What I said in it will be helpful in answering the specific points you raise:

1) "Our group leader's mistrust of us has made it virtually impossible to continue the work as we understand...."

After all these years of self-study, do you really trust yourself? If you don't, why should you demand that someone else trust you?

2) "My personal feelings of guilt in not being able to be totally candid with our group leader have produced a condition in me of seemingly being under more laws than I've ever experienced in work conditions before."

If you don't get into a situation, through work, where you experience that you are under so many laws, how will you become free? Why turn your back just because you get a result?

3) "I have come to value the effort the four of us make in the moment once a week as the most important event in my work with others at this time."

Yes, it may be, but if you do not try other kinds of work, e.g. against the Egoism which is written in big letters all through these questions (and work with your group leader is your greatest help for this), it will soon become a trap for you. One can never work just on that in the 4th Way.

4) "I see that whether I decide to leave my group leader or to stay, my thinking is affected by my personal fear of not knowing how you will deal with me if I leave."

Again the same blinding egoism; why do you think I care if you do one or the other? Your actions are your judges not I. But not a thought, I notice, for your group leader, to whom you owe everything of the Work; not a thought for the young people in the group and their needs, as I already wrote… just consuming concern for my worthless self.

I remember how Mr. and Mrs. E. arrived in Florida and their delight at finding a group forming, a short time ago. Their delight at Mr. and Mrs. N.'s arriving and being able to share this work…and already, a few months later, when you would have a real help from your relation with your group leader, and you see it shows up your enormous egoism and belief in "my understanding," "my feeling," "my inability to take a stand," etc. You want to get out and run away, with the cheap excuse that Mr. I.S. is arriving and will hold the ball, which turns out not to be so. You make the biggest mistake in your idea of a relation with your group leader — do not expect her to trust you — do not expect yourself to trust her; you will not. But try simply to relate to her, that is what is required, and to relate to her with the enormous consideration for a pupil of Mr. Gurdjieff, which is her due. Do not expect to like her — far less love her, but for her to act as a mirror for your study of your personality and your egoism — as great as hers and perhaps much greater. And try to relate to her needs, she needs you; try to relate to the group's needs, they need you. And you need them both. If you refuse this situation, where will you expect to find one you will accept?

> Love to you both... and
> my sincere wishes,
>
> Christopher Fremantle

Dear B.,

...Meanwhile try to help the group to feel the value of and action of an inner attention in bringing inner quiet and the possibility of an inner order in place of chaos. There are so many things which present themselves that it is difficult not to be drawn away from this central point....

C.F.

Mexico
7/31

Dear B.,

...It seems very wise to continue some activity through the summer; time is short really for what the Work can bring, and we need to intensify our work for this reason. One works with whoever else wishes this intensification; it cannot be imposed from outside, but it can be evoked or communicated by a kind of contagion.

...Always don't forget the crafts are a means. So easy to get involved — as tho' they are an end....

With very affectionate regards to you & R. as always,

Christopher Fremantle

Mexico
8/7/72

Dear B.,

Thank you for writing and for telling me what is happening in Chicago. You don't know for how many years I was feeling quite hopeless about the group here — and now something true and living has appeared — by that miracle which, like all life, our mind cannot understand.

If you begin to see that your life happens to you more than you think, more than you shape it (by being carried on the current to Florida), you begin to have the possibility of living in the present, more concerned with today than tomorrow. But will you really see it? Or will you go on thinking in the same way?

You should reread the part of Don Juan[19] we read...instead of criticizing what you cannot change! How to be sure of one's aim, and because one is sure of one's aim and death is there sitting with one "on the mat," one is patient and courageous, without self-pity and without fear, certain of victory because of the justice of the law that "as you sow you will reap."

In Florida you depend more on your own work in the quiet — that nourishment we need so much and neglect so much — and on your family life. It may be a

---

[19] Carlos Castañeda, *Teachings of Don Juan: The Yaqui Way of Knowledge*. University of California Press, Berkeley, 1968.

good experience. But whom will you blame when there is no group? I had this experience living quite alone in Paris! To see how all my negativeness had its origin entirely in me. I had never seen that so clearly in more than 20 years....

> With very warm and affectionate regards to you both as always,
>
> C.F.

Mexico
8/26

Dear B.,

The only way, I find, to take being with a group is to make use of it for one's own aim. You say you have experienced "another quality of work," which means you have your own impressions; they correspond to that wish in you for something. Then the challenge to work is in bringing such a state, or such a thought, or both, to a few people (or to the group), to evoke the same need in them....

Don't give way to thoughts that nobody "understands you," or that the group "wishes you'd go away." Believe in the truth.

You see how Krishnamurti must have the courage to go about lecturing, knowing that only 3 or 4% of his hearers understand him. He follows his own aim without being negative about the results. It is impossible to engage in work without finding ourselves often in that situation. We need patience and intelligence.

I had a letter from Mr. B. and M.T. about my going to N.Y. and I gave them some encouragement, as I admire their spirit of coming to Chicago from that distance; but I try never to give advice on people's personal lives unless I could know all the aspects which are relevant. They have to do what they wish and in that way they will find themselves.

You should be glad, instead of being depressed, that you can begin to pay your debt to the Work. In N.Y. one can work for oneself. Often, in these [out of town] situations, one has to work for oneself and half a dozen other people at least. If one can do it, perhaps that is payment, and it will attract a new source of help and strength in oneself or from outside....

With affectionate regards,

Christopher Fremantle

Mexico
8/7/75

Dear A.,

    I was glad you feel this correspondence has something real in it. I need it here, feeling continually my insufficiency, and all the time the great need, which it is our obligation to fulfill, for depth and life.

    What you write about, feeling able to keep a certain distance and a certain nearness in practical things, seems very familiar. It is the context of the group which brings a sharp vision of this possibility first.

    What interests me now so much is that this possibility is related to the form of inner attention which has a certain structure (in the sense of connecting the head, feelings, and body or motor part by a kind of axial connection) and therefore a certain stability.

    When my attention is here like that it naturally returns after it needs to go out. I feel I only begin to realize the need for this in myself. It is different from the surge of automatic attention in which I lose myself. I have tried to study this in the older groups in N.Y. "in the moment," and it seems to interest them all as it does me.

                              With very affectionate
                              thoughts as always,

                                        C.F.

Mexico
7/21/75

Dear A.,

All these pressures you write of to me are out of place, but how not to be displaced in myself by them, when they occur week after week. I am sure it is necessary for me, or it would not occur so regularly!

I am still a bit mystified by [your] farm-garden project, but as you say it is a great experience, especially for those who never lived, or live, but in an urban way, and who need to feel in their living that man is connected with great cosmic cycles of nature, and not only that, but dependent on them. It is the hard physical work that brings the emotion which can recognize that. Ouspensky once said in response to my questions as to why we were offered physical work: "to normalize your breathing, mainly."

I look out of the window when I wake up at the dawn light on the mountains, and feel all kinds of wonder at the Creation...I had a letter from B.T. yesterday (with his returning Mexicans) saying "I like to think I am entitled to a bit of rest at my age till I see Mme. de Salzmann and then I feel that the only way to keep young is never to stop!! I'm sure you will agree."

Many thoughts and love,

Christopher

Mexico
8/1/74

Dear A.B.,

Be careful how you imagine things, as Dr. W. warned you. A book like *The Way of the Pilgrim*,[20] probably composed by a monk in Mount Athos, is full of analogy and wisdom and certain practices; to take them literally is pure fantasy. It starts at a point far beyond where we are; the "pilgrim" is already dead to the world, symbolized by his withered arm, and is not the naive person he is superficially represented to be.

But your own feelings when you read *The Pilgrim* are real and you can trust them. Our work will bring you closer to them.

With kind regards as always.

Sincerely,

Christopher Fremantle

---

[20] Author Unknown, *The Way of the Pilgrim* (translated from the Russian by R.M. French). S.P.C.K., London, 1960.

N.Y.C.
6/18/77

Dear A.B.,

I got your letter about research into the enneagram.

Perhaps it must be remembered that such diagrams and ideas come from a mind that is not our mind, that is, from the higher centers, and they are really only accessible to us in a different state of consciousness, that is, when the necessary mind is accessible.

The kind of research you speak about is very relative. Something can be understood by research with present thought, but we must not expect very much from it. So why not do what Mrs. P. suggests, but do not think that "instruction" in the enneagram by T. or any other person can help. The problem is not the enneagram — it is to awaken.

Sincerely,

Fremantle

N.Y.C.
5/16/78

Dear A.B.,

    One must always remember, I believe, that in our ordinary "state" of consciousness it is not possible to understand many deep questions of life. This is true of the question of the nature of time; the "mind" is subject to it, and the objective mind alone can fully understand it.

    In my experience this also applies to the enneagram. I do not feel that much about them can be discovered by "studying"; but if the "study" leads to an attention which brings contact with higher mind, it serves its purpose.

With good thoughts,

Christopher Fremantle

N.Y.C.
5/25/78

Dear A.,

At the Thursday evening meeting you can bring any questions, naturally, but you cannot guarantee they will receive answers.

Work is practical — we do not, following Mr. Gurdjieff's example, spend time in useless speculations on time and the life after death.

Also he told Anna Butkovsky to "jump higher till you drop"— but does this apply to you? That was in Russia in 1916.[21] Here we are in 1978 and you are not the age she was then — please be careful.

C.F.

---

[21] Anna Butkovsky Hewitt, *With Gurdjieff in St. Petersburg and Paris*. Samuel Weiser, Inc., New York, 1978.

4/8/78

Dear J.,

The more I observe, the more I see how one reacts too much — one must quake when the ground quakes, but why such panic? The organism wishes to survive, but finally the head knows we are only temporary visitors here; so the energy is always being displaced away from its natural center, to one or another part. It is why "meditation" is necessary — to establish an awareness of a centered attention, and of the state where the many "I's" are naturally subordinated to its centered weight. They do not disappear, but simply cannot take the reaction too far, because the "center of gravity of attention" restrains them. This is the beginning of an experience corresponding to "man #4" though it is not yet a permanent state.

There is a discussion planned here for next Tuesday on the theme "Body as Support for the Psyche in Life and in Work." It interests me very much — we know the body is important, but do not see clearly enough its limitations on one side and possibilities on the other. On the one side there is self-indulgence, and on the other puritanism, excessive asceticism, etc. A period of ill-health is a great help to focus on this question. When the body needs one's energy, it will take it. Thought, emotion, will are powerless; in that area the body is autonomous. But at points where the body connects with the psyche (response to the senses, desires, inertias of the body felt as movements of energy in the psyche, temptation, conflict, slothfulness, etc.) will-action becomes crucial.

C.F.

10/1/78

Dear J.,

Unity can be based on recognizing diversity and using it, rather than fighting it. How else can we ourselves reach unity? Division, diversity, comes from the need to respond to the life around; unity is in Being, and cannot not be. How to act from Being, and not to react from the superficial levels of our conditioning?

Affectionate regards in which A. joins,

Christopher Fremantle

Paris
5/27/63

Dear E.,

    I believe it would be a good moment to give some definite task, if you have not already done so, or to remind them of the task given — to try to be "present" in front of some person they choose.

    Into my inability to do this — which is because I am not able much to be present to myself — enter all my faults, my considerations, my fears, my love to be heard and not to listen, my weak and scattered attention.

    You try very well to help them, and you have the right and a need to demand something from them, not in your own name but in the name of the Work. We are too weak to work well, and a right demand calls on those forces which are our own but which are imprisoned in us by mechanical attitudes and mechanical cares. They do not feel the demand in themselves clearly today, and for a time, until they are able, they must feel it from you, that is, from the Work....

C.F.

5/26

Dear E.,

I see the first groups do not take the exercise regarding emanations quite in the right way and you are right to warn against imagination — one cannot "see" or "form" an atmosphere. Simply it exists. I believe the main purpose of this exercise, for us, is to see and understand better how one loses energy; do not tell that, but try to help them through trying to remain within the atmosphere to see how with every thought and action the attention goes outward and energy goes out. With self-remembering this is in control and even paying attention to outside things we do not lose energy much. It is that which they could see if they observe rightly and it is a help to understand how to come to a real inner life.

It is no good to think much about the atmosphere of others, though it explains some things one can observe.

I do not know what to say about the conversation...of the second group. The direction is useful: to understand the loss of energy. But they also have to remember that every conscious effort does two things: saves and transforms energy. It is from struggle that energy comes for new control, new ability. It is always struggle between two different levels in oneself, the more interior and the more exterior, the higher and the lower.

C.F.

Paris
10/27/65

Dear E.,

I must say the questioning I do is often right, but it does not go far enough — either something distracts me or the formatory part answers and again I feel at ease. It requires an effort we are little accustomed to, to really live questions. Yet it is that alone which brings a new kind of knowledge, a new quality of thought, a new understanding.

Every meeting brings interesting questions — the relation of the work in Paris and in Mexico, one's criticism of oneself as well as other people; but these questions are raised and fall again without those who have brought them really searching the question deeply. Perhaps you can make them see that. It requires a great effort; we all fail just there.

C.F.

12/10/68

Dear E.,

One always comes back at these times to the fundamental fact, which is at the base of all "observation"—that "I" and "my state" are not the same. At some moments one can understand this so clearly; at others it is apparently impossible to separate the two awarenesses.

With the two new groups I work with, we have stayed since the start with the question of a physical awareness as the root of observation, because in this effort the idea of separation is most clear. Afterwards one can understand it in the thought and feelings clearly too, at moments. And the feeling of "presence" which is at the same time duality and unity.

C.F.

5/18

Dear E.,

I am glad the study group is doing well and I think the chapter on Purgatory[22] is the best source, combined with the scheme of materiality,[23] coming out of the Ray of Creation, which Ouspensky uses.

I feel Mr. Gurdjieff saw man as including the same exact transformations as go on in the cosmos as a whole, and vice-versa, the cosmoses the same as man. Complete man, that is, in whom both conscious shocks operate...this is the Microcosmos, and he is receiving and transforming all the levels of energy from the Macrocosmos, a parallel system to his own.

It is consciousness as well as energy, and the hierarchy of angels and archangels in *Beelzebub* represent this, governing the four quarters of the universe, as they do in traditional religions. Moses spoke with God — so received the law.

We include a part of this experience, as we are, and our experience is the stepping stone towards understanding "the laws of world creation, world maintenance" — "inner" worlds of course....

C.F.

---

[22] G.I. Gurdjieff, *Beelzebub*.
[23] G.I. Gurdjieff, *Meetings with Remarkable Men*. E.P. Dutton & Company, Inc., New York, 1963.

Dear E.,

...The elements I find most lacking in the discussions in the groups (in your absence) is a reminder of the fact that our work is based on our response to the voice of another life, another nature, which already exists in us and is calling to us, though we are so little aware.

All my efforts to awaken, all my experiments, all my "decisions" are in some way connected with this call of a finer quality, another intelligence, in me. It is something so desirable, so lovable; at the moment I hear it, and yet the next moment I forget it completely. This is my nature.

But only responding to this call can bring me to receive other influences which can completely transform my thought and my feeling, deepen and renew them, beyond my present understanding.

Someone asked R.— it was R.— "does will originate in desire?"...in a sense will is the strength that comes from this other life in us, so much more stable, so much more strong, in its laws.

I hope for good news of you soon.

With affectionate greetings,

Christopher

N.Y.C.
5/15

Dear G.,

I must say your letters are nostalgic...the time when you found a group there, new people, everything to do...and now the friction...oh how beautiful. So your group leader favors a callow lad with a gun...and he is full of himself?...So at the first scratch you all want to go off and work by yourselves in a corner — even start a new group?

But then where will the friction be? Where will you see yourselves; and what will happen to your moral fiber, conscience and being, deserting the people who really need you, both the older and the younger, but leaving them cold in the name of "your own" work?

Do not do that, G., and do not let R. or B. do it. Just work it out till you can get work again here and can leave with good conscience. I have written them one thing they can try. Try to work for the others, with them, however difficult and stony it seems. Not just for your own egotistical ideas.

Love and courage,

Christopher

Mexico
July 31, 1972

Dear J. S.,

How quickly our links with the past and with Mr. Gurdjieff seem to dissolve, leaving us with the need to renew truth which is — like man himself — only transmitted through the rebirth of its own life, and the deepening of that life. Does truth, like life, always hang by such a mere thread? One wonders...

Love from us both,

Christopher

New York
7/14/76

Dear Mrs. M.,[24]

The difficulty with books is the same as it would be with the study of medicine or nursing — you can read them all and know everything and yet, if you are a practical woman, realize that without experience you do not know — i.e., understand — anything, professionally. Hence the idea of school.

It is just the same with consciousness and the study of our own psychology related to it. This practice of self-study is not very easy. Preparation, i.e., practical experience, is necessary. A "school," in the full sense, is a rare thing, and can only be approached in this way.

In the meantime, you have a pile of related books on your desk; why not continue to delve into them? Do they include *All and Everything*, now in paperback in three volumes? He writes about religion in one chapter and discusses it in various places — but this approach is not as close to your approach as in *In Search*, where he was talking to Russian Orthodox Christians.

Sincerely,

Christopher Fremantle

---

[24] Mrs. J.M. never met Christopher Fremantle in person; she initially received Mr. Gurdjieff's teaching through these letters.

Mexico
July 30, 1976

Dear J.M.,

You ask about "schools"... there are many levels. But what Gurdjieff spoke of was something starting "above the level of ordinary life," and taking its origin from another School, i.e., having knowledge coming from another level. This implies that any group of people who get together to study some ideas in books (even esoteric) are not necessarily a school — and that preparation is necessary — that is, individual self-study, under adequate guidance.

The idea of "intentional" or "voluntary" suffering is the last in the Work — and it implies the ability to be free from the automatic need to evade, reject, or react mechanically to suffering. This freedom cannot be acquired without a change of state and long self-study, evidently.

The relationship with one's parents, or those close to one, is most precious in the Work. To try to act as one "should" toward a relationship which is so real and undeniable, to be sincere with oneself, inevitably reveals much about oneself: one's limitations, one's conditioning through life, one's lack of inner freedom and inability to "love," etc. etc.

With warm regards, sincerely,

Christopher Fremantle

New York
September 11th, 1976

Dear J.M.,

    I am interested by your comments on the nursing and teaching professions, which you have had experience in — and also that of marriage, since you are reconsidering that relationship too at this moment.

    It is possible to see the real *profession* of mankind as evolution, personal and therefore aiding in the general evolution. Mr. Gurdjieff wrote so much on the senselessness of war, the arising and disappearance of true "culture," in *All and Everything*, and of the struggle to rediscover its foundations, in *Meetings with Remarkable Men*. (Yes — the "3rd Series" *will* mean more to you if you read it later.)

    If you see this as a truth, then one cannot help seeing that every "profession" in life reflects the inner conflict, disorder and imperfection in ourselves, and it follows that while a "change" will be only a change of context, the real change will be in making any profession serve as a means of awakening and personal evolution.

With sincere regards,
yours,

Christopher Fremantle

41 E. 59
N.Y.C. 10022
1/30/77

Dear J.M.,

Thank you for your letter describing your attempts to make a practical work in your everyday life. They all seem to be positive and well directed.

You are right to work in several directions at once; life is too short to take only one study at a time. To the ones you enumerate you might add: to observe your postures and gestures — which often help to know your inner state, because they often reflect it, as well as aspects of personality.

While you take several studies at once, make one your *special* study or task, for one or two weeks — then another one; this way you refresh your interest in new discovery.

Try to be clear for yourself on *your own personal impulse*, your personal wish and aim; no one else can give you theirs.

Some reading, as you mention, is good; but do not read too much — you yourself are the book to study — everything is there.

Best wishes for 1977 and hoping to hear again from you,

Christopher Fremantle

N.Y.
2/26/77

Dear J.M.,

Do not be deceived by the discovery of "new dark corners" and feeling you have "lost a lot of ground." This is the result of seeing some inner things one was not aware of clearly before. Nothing changes so easily, not for the worse or the better.

So pursue the self-observation and self-remembering — it is the essence of the way change can come about — and will provide the energy and right vision for change... So you are "not discouraged"! That is the *only* attitude — to follow one's aim whatever the circumstances, with courage and without doubt or weakness. I am glad your present life seems to bring you help — children are never fooled and are excellent mirrors in which to see oneself!

With all good wishes and please write again when you have time.

Sincerely,

Christopher Fremantle

New York City
April 3, 1978

Dear J.M.,

You are concerned about your son receiving good influences of the Teaching. What may be important to understand is that all the time, day and night, a person "emanates" in accordance with his state, unconsciously.

So a child is affected by the moods, joys and sorrows of his parents, for better or worse, so strongly. At the same time, it is only an adult who can judge and receive "ideas" as they appear in books, and work from them.

So to work on yourself is the best way to help him — to try to be *conscious*, not to try to "change" or to criticize yourself, or to "influence" him. Just to be able to be positive and joyous, not identified and lost in small things, nor to be mean or petty, which is already asking a great deal from oneself.

As you say, try to see, more and more, your *automatic reactions* — you will be glad later on — it is the shortest way to freedom.

It is too soon to try to understand the relation of sex to inner development; you have to study *all* automatism for now.

With very kind regards and good wishes.

Sincerely,

Christopher Fremantle

July 5th, 1978

Dear J.M.,

It requires some decision and courage to undertake serious self-study without support from at least a few others working on the same line; one sees, as you say, many things relating to less attractive aspects of life around one, and that they are there in me too. It is not an easy experience and being shared with others one can better see that this is, after all, the human situation. So one needs, too, an aim to come into a different way of living and being, through that study; otherwise the negative side may seem too much. One has the impression that things are "worse than before," but it is not true!

I am interested to see how you find your baby a help to see yourself; one excuses oneself to oneself for irritation and ill humor, but to offer these emanations to an infant who has no recourse makes one feel, as you say, a real remorse. It is principally this remorse which Gurdjieff saw as bringing about change — gradually. Today, he said, is the result of yesterday; tomorrow will be like today, if there is nothing done "now" — "today." Then if something is done, tomorrow will be different. He said to try to feel remorse for one's bad manifestations; "repair the past; prepare the future!"

"Seeing" one's faults, in the sense of really experiencing them at the moment of action, when often repeated, itself brings the cure — one can no longer hurt another when it is clearly seen that one does so.

...The baby, waking at night and demanding, also is a help. The body should be a good servant and should be able to wake, sleep, carry and fetch as needed; in return you must give it justice and supply its needs of food and sleep and so on, without indulgence or neglect. The small child teaches one to be available even when the body protests, showing that it is there to serve the human spirit, not interfere.

As you imply, the time of the last stages of carrying a child are difficult for both parents; for the mother, in ways you experienced; for the father, also difficult, often because the energies associated with sex do not have their usual flow, and tend to go into the thought, feeling and so on. This may make a man more sensitive, and exaggerate his moods and desires. It is a difficult time; I know from experience.

You ask some other questions about the sex relationship. It is very important because it plays such a vital part in human relationships; but it seems to me that Gurdjieff considered it could only be understood and helped later, after the working of the more accessible centers — motor, thought, emotions, body and instinct — had been studied and to a certain extent "normalized" or raised to a higher level. Because effectively, we hardly see the action of sex itself. Chiefly we see its physical, emotional, mental, etc., results in ourselves; cleansing these parts will also help to normalize sex. For example, nothing is so antipathetic to a good sexual relationship as ill-humor, irritation and so on, which may use up the energies that sex requires. Self-pity can do the same. It burns up the energies love requires, and paralyses it.

For the moment try to observe always what really takes place in life, in all one's interactions with the life around. Life is the best teacher. To observe oneself is much less easy than people imagine — Gurdjieff said it is enough for several years; but it is always there, and sometimes books will bring one a fresh impulse; sometimes one's family will; sometimes the "teaching" itself.

Write when you have time.

> All good wishes and
> sincere regards,
>
> Christopher Fremantle

178 E. 90th
12/3/78

Dear E.,

    I address you with the request that you pass on to all those named in the note I received this evening, with the lovely cactus, how touched I was by the thought — as though something had remained with us, from a few years of often dry, hard meetings, of the humility and simplicity in Mr. Gurdjieff's presence.

    The rose garden is only reached through the desert, after many years. But Providence gives even the poorest plant, like this one, the means for survival in itself, the continuing life.

    I am afraid it will be, at best, the new year before I am able to join you again regularly, but I am on the road to improvement again, and look forward with special warmth to the time —

                                    Thank you again from my heart,

                                    Christopher Fremantle

Sunrise Bookshop
3054 Telegraph
Berkeley, California 94705

Date: 11/05/07

Reg. No.	Clerk	Account Forward	
1	ON ATTENTION		
2	FROMMITE	30 w	
3			
4		R	2.65
5			32.65
6			
7			
8			
9			
10			
11			
12			
13			
14	3225-23		
15			

THANK YOU
Call Again

We appreciate your patronage and
hope we may continue to merit it.
If we please you, tell your friends.
If we don't, tell us.
We strive to satisfy.